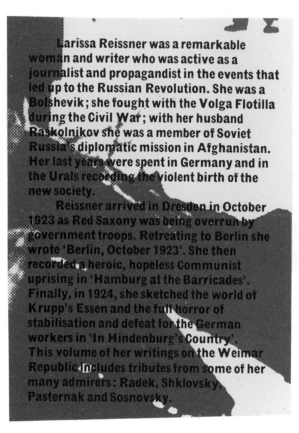

Larissa Reissner was a remarkable woman and writer who was active as a journalist and propagandist in the events that led up to the Russian Revolution. She was a Bolshevik; she fought with the Volga Flotilla during the Civil War; with her husband Raskolnikov she was a member of Soviet Russia's diplomatic mission in Afghanistan. Her last years were spent in Germany and in the Urals recording the violent birth of the new society.

Reissner arrived in Dresden in October 1923 as Red Saxony was being overrun by government troops. Retreating to Berlin she wrote 'Berlin, October 1923'. She then recorded a heroic, hopeless Communist uprising in 'Hamburg at the Barricades'. Finally, in 1924, she sketched the world of Krupp's Essen and the full horror of stabilisation and defeat for the German workers in 'In Hindenburg's Country'. This volume of her writings on the Weimar Republic includes tributes from some of her many admirers: Radek, Shklovsky, Pasternak and Sosnovsky.

REĬSNER, Larissa Mikhaĭlovna. Hamburg at the barricades, and other writings on Weimar Germany, by Larissa Reissner. tr. from the Russian and ed. by Richard Chappell. Urizen (dist. by Dutton), 1977. 209p maps. 8.95 ISBN 0-904383-36-9

CHOICE   DEC. '77
History, Geography &
Travel

Europe

Larissa Reissner (1895–1926) was born in Russia of Baltic-German and Polish parentage. She became an early sympathizer and later follower of the Bolsheviks, and devoted much of her journalistic work and talent to relating the events of the abortive German Communist revolutions to Russian readers. Translated largely from Russian texts, her accounts offer interesting vignettes of people and places, of the suppression of the Reds in Saxony, the Communist uprising in Hamburg in 1923, and the subdued atmosphere of the Ruhr region. In a lively style, the translations seem to capture the spirit of the original writings. Reissner's contributions give insights into the mood and atmosphere of the events but are limited in relating concrete historical information. The volume concludes with tributes from Karl Radek, whose reputed mistress Larissa had been, Victor Shklovsky, Boris Pasternak, and Lev Sosnovsky. Recommended for university libraries with very strong German history collections. No index or bibliography.

LARISSA REISSNER

HAMBURG AT THE BARRICADES

and other writings
on Weimar Germany

translated from the Russian
and edited by
Richard Chappell

First published 1977
by Pluto Press Limited
Unit 10 Spencer Court
7 Chalcot Road, London NW1 8LH

Copyright © Pluto Press 1977

ISBN 0 904383 36 9

Typeset by Preface Limited, Salisbury
Printed by The Camelot Press Limited, Southampton
Maps by Joyce Batey
Designed by Richard Hollis, GrR
Cover designed by David King

Contents

Germany in 1923

In Memory of

GEORG JUNGCLAS

Sixty Years
a Revolutionary Internationalist
Halberstadt, 22 February 1902
Cologne, 11 September 1975

Editorial Note

Sources

Berlin, October 1923 (Berlin v oktyabre 1923 goda) was first published by the M.O.P.R. (International Organisation for Revolutionary Fighters' Aid), Moscow 1924, as an appendix to *Hamburg at the Barricades*.

Hamburg at the Barricades (Gamburg na barrikadakh) first appeared in the journal *Zhizn* no.1,1924 although without the last chapter. Extracts were printed in *Izvestia* no.40, 1924 (under the title 'Hamburg – Free City') and in *Molodoi Leninets*, 25 and 29 October 1924 (under the title of 'Barmbeck in Struggle'). It was first issued in book form by M.O.P.R. in 1924 in the edition referred to above. Further extracts were later published in *Molodoi Leninets*, 27 February 1926 (under the title 'Hamm') and in the book *In the Battles for the World October* published in Moscow in 1932 (under the title 'Elfriede from Schiffbek'). A film entitled *Hamburg* based upon the book was made at the V.U.F.K.U. studios in 1926 with script by S.Schreiber and Y.Yanovsky and directed by Ballyuzek.

The sketches that make up *In Hindenburg's Country* were first published in *Izvestia* nos.185,187, 194, 201 and 227, 1925. Not included in this series were 'Frau Fritzke', 'Slippers', and 'He a Communist and she a Catholic' which first appeared in the book version

9

of the sketches entitled *In Hindenburg's Country: Sketches of Contemporary Germany (V strane Gindenburga: ocherki sovremennoi Germanii)* published by *Pravda*, Moscow 1926. 'In the Ruhr – Under the Ground' was not included in this edition.

'Milk' was first published in the newspaper *Gudok* no.258, 1925.

All these works have been reprinted in various collections of Larissa Reissner's writings published subsequently in the USSR namely, the *Sobranie Sochinenii* (in two volumes but by no means a complete edition) of 1928, the *Izbrannye Proizvedeniya* of 1958 and the *Izbrannoe* of 1965. 'Junkers' has been omitted from the last two editions. A short passage in 'Krupp and Essen' referring to Karakhan's diplomatic work in China has been cut out of the two post-war editions.

A German translation of *Hamburg at the Barricades (Hamburg auf den Barrikaden: Erlebtes und Erhörtes aus dem Hamburger Aufstand 1923)* was published by Neue Deutsche Verlag of Berlin in 1925 but without the last chapter. In 1926 the same publisher issued a collection of the author's work entitled *Oktober* with the translator given as Eduard Scheimann. This included the *Hindenburg* sketches with the exception of 'In the Ruhr – Under the Ground' and 'He a Communist and she a Catholic' and contained a special preface to *In Hindenburg's Country* which was given the subtitle 'A Journey through the German Republic 1924'. *Oktober* was re-issued in 1930 with some of the contents slightly re-arranged. A further collection in German translation, that included the Berlin and Hamburg sketches as well, was published by Dietz of Berlin in 1960.

By far the most detailed, though incomplete, bibliography of Larissa Reissner's work and critical articles on her can be found in *Sovetskie Pisateli: Prozaiki*, volume 7 part 2, Moscow 1972, pp. 65–83.

The texts used for the translations in this edition are as follows:

Berlin, October 1923 in *Izbrannoe* 1965
Hamburg at the Barricades (except 'German Mensheviks After the Rising') in *Zhizn* 1924

'German Mensheviks After the Rising' in *Izbrannoe* 1965
In Hindenburg's Country, Preface to the German Edition; *Oktober* 1926; 'Krupp and Essen', 'The Barracks and a Cobbler's Wife', 'An Iron Cross', 'In the Ruhr – Under the Ground', 'Ullstein' and 'Junkers', in *Izvestia* 1925; 'Frau Fritzke', 'Slippers' and 'He a Communist and she a Catholic' in *Sobranie Sochinenii* 1928; 'Milk' in *Izbrannoe* 1965

'Larissa Reissner': K.Radek, foreword to L.Reissner, *Sobranie Sochinenii*, Moscow 1928
'A Most Absurd Death': V.Shklovsky, *Gamburgskii Schet*, Moscow, 1928
'In Memory of Reissner': B.Pasternak, *Stikhotvoreniya i Poemy*, Moscow 1965
'In Memory of Larissa Reissner': L.Sosnovsky, *Lyudi Nashego Vremeni*, Moscow 1927

German words in the original Russian text have been translated in parenthesis.

Identities in 'Hamburg at the Barricades'

Radek, in his article printed in the appendix to this volume recounts the peculiar circumstances in which *Hamburg at the Barricades* was written. Because of the police persecution of Hamburg communists and insurgents Larissa protected the identity of most of the participants she writes about referring to them by initials only. The first German edition was even less specific, using only X. or 'a comrade' to denote individual fighters. The personal anecdotes about K. and the scene of the respite in a Barmbeck pub were also omitted from that edition presumably for security reasons.

Of the three men who formed the effective staff in Barmbeck, T., C. and Kb, only T. is identified in later Soviet editions as Ernst Thälmann. Ruth Fischer in her *Stalin and German Communism* (New York 1948) names the leader of the unsuccessful assault on Von-Essen Strasse police station as Hans Botzenhardt, the man referred to by Larissa as C. Kb could possibly be Hans Kippenberger, the head of the Communist Party's military organisation in and Kippenberger's account of the Von-Essen Strasse attack and of the course of the rising as a whole (see A.Neuberg: *Armed Insurrection*, London 1970) suggests that Kippenberger might have been the unnamed leader whom Radek tells us Larissa checked her material with when she returned to Moscow early in 1924; for Kippenberger had taken refuge there and wrote his own account in May of that year.

The leading figure in the rising at Schiffbek was, according to one later account, Fiete Schule: possibly he is Larissa's S.

Richard Krebs's memoirs (Jan Valtin, *Out of the Night*, Toronto 1941) unfortunately shed no clear light on any of these figures. The other published memoirs of an insurgent (W.Zeutschel, *Im Dienst der Kommunistische Terrororganisation*, Berlin 1931) are, according to Ruth Fischer, excessively romanticised and unreliable in detail although their author did himself take part in the Von-Essen Strasse assault under the alias of Burmeister.

Some more recent scholarly works appear to be unhelpful. Heinz Habedank's monograph *Zur Geschichte des Hamburger Aufstandes 1923* (Berlin 1958) concentrates on the supposedly decisive role of Thälmann, and also of Stalin (sic), but does not once mention Kippenberger's part let alone that of any other particular individuals. Werner T.Angress in his *Stillborn Revolution* (Princeton 1963) is exclusively concerned with how the order for the rising came to be given. He also states incorrectly that Larissa Reissner was an eye-witness.

As an antidote to the invariably inaccurate and trite footnotes that Larissa's life and work has provoked in the available material on early Soviet history and literature we append to this, the first English edition of her writings, a selection of more considered appreciations made by distinguished friends and contemporaries.

In 1937 the poet Osip Mandelstham remarked that Larissa was lucky to have died in time: all the people in her circle, as he put it, were being 'destroyed wholesale' by then. At her funeral on 11 February 1926 the coffin was borne by Radek, Boris Volin, Enukidze, Lashevich, I.N.Smirnov and Pilnyak. Four of them were murdered by Stalin's bureaucracy some ten years later while Lashevich, like Larissa, 'died in time'. Hermann Remmele, the communist leader referred to in *Berlin, October 1923*, Lev Sosnovsky, the writer of the final appreciation included in this volume and Karakhan, the Soviet envoy to China alluded to in 'Krupp and Essen' were also shot in that slaughter. And as Hans Kippenberger stepped off his train in Moscow in 1936 he was arrested as a 'Reichswehr agent' and executed.

I would like to record my thanks to the following people who in different ways have given valuable assistance, advice and encouragement in the production of this book: John Archer, Patrick Goode, Colin Ham, Iwan Majstrenko, David Zane Mairowitz, Hermann Müller, Ann Pasternak Slater, Anthony van der Poorten and Anita Wisniewska.

I have also with great personal sorrow to acknowledge the unique contribution made to this and earlier jobs by my mother, Winifred L.Chappell, whose unexpected death I learnt of as this book was in the final stages of preparation. Over a period of years she readily brought the mind of an unusually versatile linguist and dedicated teacher to bear on any fine point of translation, though always offering any suggestion with the great prudence and modesty so natural to her.

May I also take this opportunity to express my appreciation of the courteous and helpful way the staff at the library of the School of Slavonic and East European Studies, London, and the British Library have treated my requests and queries.

R.C.

Berlin, October 1923

In the Reichstag

What a parliament! If there is anything in it that can inspire respect it can only be Wilhelm I's enormous marble boots standing in the middle of the hall. The old soldier, from whom a constitution had been wrung with such difficulty in his time, stands there with a disapproving look and awaits the moment when he will be allowed to drive the chattering flocks of deputies out of this house. The members of parliament peacefully swarm around his celebrated jackboots, promenading singly and in couples exactly like girls on the boulevard. From time to time their carefree crowds are parted by an elderly functionary leading a few youths clad in thick woollen stockings and hobnailed boots who have come, sweating from this act of homage, to look over the House of the German People. Screwing up their school caps, the youths servilely and bashfully eye the oaken maidens with gilt navels that hold up the ceiling, the torrents of frock-coats and those most excellent old footmen who represent, like some lofty personage writing his memoirs, the only bearers of the old parliamentary traditions. Alas, no traces and no semblance of former grandeur! Not a single major figure who can attract even the respectful hatred of all parties. Not a single man distinguished for his personal integrity or for having a few decades of untarnished political gaming behind him. When old Bebel passed through this hall his enemies would stand up and even die-hard Prussian Junkers would clumsily raise themselves out of their swampy armchairs to acknowledge his clean name; today — no one, not one face nor one name. There in the fog of tobacco smoke is the insignificant profile of Levi, a grey, reserved face that has been trained without stage make-up to endure the curiosity of people scrutinising it with their private thoughts about the treachery that he committed. Everything is from the past; members of previous ministries thrown into convulsions by public disgust, belching statesmen, yesterday's men retaining for all time the stains of an indelible filth on the tails of their deputies' outfits.

By and large it is easy to pick several basic types of parliamentary fauna out of the crowd. In the first place there are those who have already been put to use, occupying ministerial posts and managing to fill in their obscure names on some international form or on one of the tearful pleas addressed to the Entente. Here are the socialists renowned for shooting down workers and cabinet members who took on the responsibility of plundering the gold reserves of the German republic — in short, men who have been put into mass circulation.

The pattern on the back of the cards is well-known to every regular player. Never again when a cabinet is being formed will the hand of a great card-sharp pick them up and never again will he lay out Grand Coalitions on the table. The card that has once been taken out of a player's hand and thrown back in his face, a beaten and abused card, continues to live on as a back-bencher. But his great days are past. Scattered across the Reichstag's red carpet is a great multitude of these assorted played-out hands. They continue to vote but the younger enthusiasts who have not yet lost their political virginity reach forward for the political honours. Behind the backs of the old buccaneers passing by they recall with awe and envy the sums of the hand-outs the former had received, their imaginative betrayals and their dazzling scandals. A gallery of disgraced, crumpled physiognomies that had however managed to sip from the cup of sweet power in good time. They, the naked among the naked, walk about with no sense of shame. Among these has-beens swarms of the more mobile, stupid and persistent gather:

they are the rulers of tomorrow. A whole flight of them buzzes and clusters round Breitscheid who is surrounded by the flower of political camp-followers. Just very slightly like a black market but for the most part sweet-sounding, fragrant and well modulated. Here too the pride and the adornment of the Reichstag — almost its only woman political correspondent, a tiny black miscarriage wrapped up in the sheet of an indecent little stock exchange bulletin — is being put to pasture. The Rights walk about as if at the races. White gaiters, spangles of glass under their arched brows and the triangle of a handkerchief against the chest. In their half of the buffet, which is completely separate from the Democratic Party's feeding-trough, they pass up and down as if in a salon where there is no risk of encountering anything ignoble. However, right alongside the aristocratic, stiff, hideous, haughty genuinely Prussian ladies who have the habit of taking their five o'clock tea amid the fug of political tittle-tattle, treading on their furs and trailing withered tails like old lizards, there also roll in the plump banking and industrial patriots who are so fat and garrulous that the pages of the black *Crusader News* sticking out of the right-wing deputies' pockets ought to be bent round and the crosses on them, Christian-Fascist crosses, turned right round. Alas, these are now the money bags, and the luncheons they gorge during the intervals in the performance are more copious, nourishing and expensive than those that sustain the pedigree Junkers.

At the tables of the Social-Democratic Party there are sausages, coffee and anxieties. All the Reichstag's entrances and exits have been cordoned off. The police grab every passer-by by the scruff of the neck; in the doorways stand the most senior footmen, eunuchs of the political harem who, knowing the face of each one of its legal wives and each one of its favourite concubines, check with their own hands and let through the representatives of the people. Inside, by the newspaper kiosk, there stands a jolly, strapping fellow, the Berlin Chief of Police who pins his clear searching look on every deputy's face to try to detect the criminal element. Messrs. delegates put on an open honest face and rush past him about their business. Yet, in spite of all the precautions, the communists will suddenly create some scene. A completely absurd, panic-stricken fear that Remmele will suddenly burst in, cause an affray, toss a smoke bomb in and blow up the whole Reichstag. Remmele's name is repeated like an obsession. His appearance is awaited like a *coup de théâtre*. It is chewed over, swallowed, belched up and swallowed once more. Yet were that Remmele to appear now with even a gramophone horn or the stone NCO to give a cough from his marble stump this parliament would disperse in shame. General Seeckt knows this too and so for the moment does not make the classic knee movement, a gesture described with such marvellous vividness in Voltaire's *Candide*.

The game of parliament has no relation to the fate of Germany and her revolution. History, like the huge statues standing by the fountain in front of the Reichstag, has long since turned its cast-iron backside upon it.

And so they plot, bargain and battle for power.

For power. Are you laughing, General Seeckt? Or isn't it so? Power has long since left that tall house; but the tiresome, relentless, indestructible swarms of politicking philistines still gather around the greasy marks left by previous deputies' unwashed hands on the pages of the constitution. Like flies. One black, screwed up, rejected slip of paper has been left behind yet they plaster it, crawl over it and buzz round it . . .

The debating chamber. Someone speaks. A burst of laughter. He is answered from the right. Prolonged, jubilant laughter. Cries from the left. Hollow cynical laughter. That is the opening performance at the German Reichstag, its great day.

Workers' Children

Berlin is starving. In the street every day people who have fainted from exhaustion are being picked up on the trams and in the queues. Starving drivers drive the trams, starving motormen urge their trains on along the infernal corridors of the underground, starving men go off to work or roam without work for days and nights around the parks and the city's outlying areas.

Starvation hangs on the buses, shutting its eyes on the spinning staircase to the upper deck while advertisements, desolation and motor horns reel past like drunks. Starvation stands guard over Wertheim's majestic counters, taking in twenty thousand million a week when a pound of bread costs roughly ten thousand million. Starvation serves fussily and attentively in the hundreds of deserted department stores that are crammed with riches, golden in the light and as clean and as respectable as the international banks. That young miss on whose pointed triangle of a face there are only bluish recesses for eyes, a little powder and an obsequious smile, points like a hunting dog to some 10-dollar boots and a 30-dollar rug. While faint with hunger she is selling herself for a penny ha'penny at the old rate and yet she can calculate with a purely German thoroughness and at lightning speed the speculator's billions and trillions, enter them in the account in that exquisite handwriting possessed by this entire nation of highly literate people; as she waits for the next round of staff cuts, she resignedly undoes her shop assistant's overall but still without daring to detach that fawning hungry smile from her face.

The walls of the huge blocks that turn their bare backs to the windows of the trains flying past are painted with advertisements in which yesterday's accumulated surplus of production exclaims and exults, gulping down sweet grease from a tin of condensed milk while giant children with round, rosy cheeks like buttocks and happy blond smiles raise lamp-post-like bars of chocolate aloft over the city. But the real, living children have stopped going to school because of hunger: the mothers take them along and ask the teacher to let them go home if they start to feel bad during lessons. For how can a small child last through the classes if it has had nothing to eat either that morning or the night before?

In the last months infant mortality has made a sudden, high leap on the black charts of German statistics. Thick tubercular spittle clings to the life of such districts as Wedding, Riksdorf and Oberschöneweide, the seats of power of AEG electricity and the motor corporations, and the scenes of the most massive lock-outs conducted under artillery cover and of the first thousands-strong meetings where in these early October days so unlike ours, German workers are learning to sing the 'Internationale'. This late European autumn that so slowly wanes and so hesitantly freezes the clear Berlin nights has carried away thousands of workers' children. At no time since the war has lobar pneumonia eaten away so many lives, spitting and coughing themselves out drop by drop in the bread queues or whiling away the hours of fever, asphyxia and starvation in the never-ending strolls of unemployment.

Unemployed! Not for weeks, not for months but for a year or even more. And with it of course, the wife, the three or four children and all the hundred and one misfortunes that burst into a man's life when he is already down, worn out and torn to shreds; sickness, incapacity for work or some involuntary weakness at the crucial moment in the wild scramble for the chance piece of bread that turns up. But however crying their need, the lowest layers of petty-bourgeois, utterly ruined and deprived of all means of subsistence, still manage to bend and to try to adapt themselves and some-how overcome the 'hard times'. They economise and hoard the money that by tomorrow will have turned into a pile of rubbish, stinting themselves in every way if only to keep up the appearance of a poor, but decent, life of toil. Living in poverty, working for abso-lutely nothing and yet, as they clutch at the cashier's grills from which every three days a new derisory sum is spat out, sensing the soothing silence of a fireproof safe stuffed full of the boss's money between themselves and the threatening revolution. Ready for any-thing if only to avoid the social revolution. Hence that handful of dictators, those lengthy discussions in the newspapers about the true badge of a dictator and those portraits of high-cheekboned, large-muzzled generals of the Wilhelmine era. The petty bourgeois is still hoping that one of the marble idiots that stand with arms pre-sented in the Siegesallee will come to deliver the German people from left-wing anarchy and right-wing putsches and economic rui-nation. Although such a desperation has set in amid Germany's fine, civilised, asphalt-carpeted cities that the soul of the little clerk, the office-worker and the public official is ready to go on all fours and howl like an animal, he or she will at the last minute go not on to the streets but to the cafe. Yes, to the cafe for a thimbleful of coffee in exchange for the financial left-overs of the whole week, to bemuse his swollen, healthy anger with a damp, reeling waltz, the gilt of little bow-legged baroque tables and the illusions of tobacco smoke, saccharine and courtesans' hats.

Every one of the most humble office-workers and even of the top-grade skilled workers invariably has his own furniture in his flat, gathered over a lifetime of rigorous economising and self-denial. Several soft armchairs, rugs with the Holy Scriptures on them, a winged angel, bunches of dried grasses and always a *Vertiko*, a sort of truncated cabinet, that altar to middle-class cosiness on which there stands the family portraits, a statuette that is indecent when viewed from below and the wedding bouquet under a bell-glass. But until such time as the usurious policy of the bourgeoisie takes the *Vertiko* and the five padded-backed armchairs away and removes the heavy curtains that hang like huge velvet trousers from the windows, their owner will not go out on to the street nor abandon hope of that peaceful, bloodless overturn that for fifty years now the Social-Democratic Party has called for at the expense of the German proletariat.

But where there is no *Vertiko* there is no money or bread either, for in the real depths of the working class while the husband spends his unemployed hours walking the streets, the mother moves round one philanthropic institution after another. If she is pregnant in addition, the doctor will carefully examine her heavy tummy and an equally hungry but highly respectable nurse will enter the unborn child in the register of the poor, give it a number and inform her that in about two months' time it might be possible to get hold of milk for the infant at twenty-five per cent off the market price.

An unemployed man's wife who is pregnant now, in the winter of 1923, is a corpse.

She lies slumped on the chair, her belly sticking out from her dark, hungry, decaying body just as if a child's round head has been, for some reason, hidden in her lap under her dress. Even the philanthropic young lady is not quite at her ease at the sight of this living woman with her living and already visible child, both of whom will certainly no longer be living in a matter of three months, not having the slightest chance of lasting out this winter in a country where the unemployed receives sixty thousand million a week while a pound of bread cost eighty the day before yesterday, a hundred and sixty yesterday and tomorrow may soar to three hundred. She and her husband have been unemployed since last January, that is for ten whole months. This January, right at the coldest and most terrible time, he will stop receiving benefit altogether. And that's with four children.

"Why didn't your husband go and work during the summer and dig potatoes with the farmers?"

"He did, but injured his foot. He spent all summer in hospital with blood poisoning."

In such cases misfortune knows no bounds and no reasonable limit but tumbles in an absurdly hopeless heap on to the heads of those already weakened. She has tuberculosis without a doubt: noisy difficult breathing as if asleep.

"So where do you want to have it? At home or in the hospital?"

"At home."

Wisely, the doctor for a while tries to dissuade her, tempting her with the cleanliness, warmth and food.

In the end with a quite unexpected and irresistible smile:

"Doctor, I want to die at home. I want my husband to see the child and wrap it up in the linen himself."

Another woman: two plaits like ears of rye around a young head, a white neck and a shawl tied across her full figure.

A jolly woman as clean and as strong as the hand-woven linen laid out to dry in the mountain sun of the Black Forest or Bavaria. Out of work for a year and two months. Her husband who brought her here is waiting in the hall. She wears a strikingly clean blouse washed in cold water without soap; large, healthy teeth keep flashing in her generous, cherry-lipped smile.

In reply to the question put by a yellowing sister furrowed with wrinkles like old-fashioned gothic handwriting, "What will you live on in the winter?" she says:

"I don't know. Either we'll pass out or everything'll change."

Two girls. Both unemployed. Both pregnant. One is swollen with the tears that accompany reproaches and hunger. The younger one, a frank-looking child indifferent to everything, is brought in by her tiny irate mother wearing a fancy hat and carrying a reticule. The sister purses her thin lips and wants to close the door through to the waiting room to avoiding broadcasting the disgrace.

"*Quatsch!* (Rubbish!) There's no need. We're making workers not those that we'd like to see dead."

The most downtrodden German working woman supports her children, her ruined, plundered home and her pauperised, unemployed family with an inconceivable strength.

The whole family has been starving: it has been starving

for months. But as long as there remains the least possibility, the baby will have a quarter of a bottle of milk and fifty grams of gruel. Living in one room are five or six people, two of whom have tuberculosis, but the baby that the mother takes for an examination every week without fail is immaculately clean and wrapped up in a clean piece of cloth. Only very gradually, over six months and when the family that has been holding it up on outstretched arms high above its own poverty, finally subsides into the morass of starvation, only then will the colour leave its face, its weakened bones protrude more sharply beneath its thin, greying skin and the doctor's fingers feel the soft, swollen and slowly closing skull under the light matted crop of hair. In each workers' hospital (and there are dozens of them) pointers record the unabating weight loss of thousands of working-class children every day. On these scales lies an entire proletarian generation, squealing, waggling their thin little legs in the air and twisting their weak toothless mouths from side to side; as they become ever lighter and ever paler they drain away amid sickly infants' tears and the yellow froth of starvation's diarrhoea. Germany's working class has not been and will not be defeated. But today, just as its forces are still being collected into a strong communist fist, the struggle against it is waged by the most contemptible means, that is, by striking above all at the future of the working class, its children. And here the German proletarian woman has risen to her full stature in their defence.

Very often a man just cannot stand the ravages of hunger, the screaming of unfed children, the starvation and the filth. Thousands of working women are abandoned by their husbands and lovers after a few months of unemployment. It is easy to spot in a crowd of others the woman who is pursuing the frantic struggle for survival at her own risk and peril by her peculiarly ashen face, the marks of a convulsed overstrain and her grimy bloodless head, shrunken into a fist-like shape. From her, and only from her, can the experienced eye tell whether unemployment started long ago or recently, and whether it has been interrupted by occasional earnings for two or three days or four to six hours. For the baby of the woman who has just started to go hungry and the baby whose little head flops to one side through weakness while the ominous ulcers that exhaustion brings have already appeared behind its ears, under its armpits and between its legs are identically clean, licked, laid out on pillows and covered up with their mother's warm shawl. In the end, though, you can get nowhere with just doctor's orders and painstaking care. They have to be fed and milk has to be bought. Medicines have to be ordered when the first sores appear on the baby's feeble body.

It begins with little trifles: scrofulous inflammations, a patch of moist skin that has to be disinfected and powdered. The sickness spreads and embraces the whole organism. Lying in nappies is a little old man of seven or eight months with an inflamed mouth, the bridge of his nose depressed, bowed legs and a pot belly. His excrement smells putrid.

That is the end of many months' heroic struggle. A freak instead of a strong, well-formed healthy baby.

Every one of the unemployed mothers who comes invariably to the hospital each week knows that sooner or later it must end like that. She knows this and yet nevertheless fights — with all the technical means that science teaches for the fight against starvation and degeneration.

With all the forces of youth and love and all the grit and culture of the only working class in the world in whose ranks there are no illiterate men or illiterate mothers either.

When he has finished his examination of the child, the doctor turns to the mother:

"Show me your breasts."

Under her dress there is not even a vest. But at the first touch warm white blood splashes from the high over-full nipple on to the papers and the doctor's glasses and apron.

A Prosperous Worker's Family

The elephant pokes his trunk through the bars of the grille and for a few second looks at our Hilda with wise and hungry eyes. No, she's not going to give him anything!

That wisest of the wise goes off into the back of his cage rustling his dry skin white with age and flapping his ears despondently. The zoo is empty and cold and the animals are starving like the people. The elephant will die soon, that is obvious from its ribs and flaccid trunk. A complete skeleton, a complete zoological specimen of a wild beast that has spent a hundred years standing in the middle of a museum yet can still walk and eat a little hay. This specimen, which has yet to reach the moment of expiration, is still draped in the rustling folds of his old skin until the unveiling. Hilda is at first very scared and shuts her eyes. But after taking a peep, she asks: "Do tell me, does he have a face?" Then she touches the cold brass rail and feels quite secure when she knows that the mountain is sitting in a prison.

"Uncle, isn't he sweet!"

Some Russian emigres standing in front of the monkey-house offering empty matchboxes, pieces of litter and dog-ends to the clever old baboon. He is deeply annoyed; catching the sound of somebody's family squabble inside the pavilion he strains his ears with human curiosity and then runs off to join the scene, slamming the little door and presenting the bluish-purple part of his anatomy to our Russian fellow-countrymen.

"Let's move a bit quicker, Hilda, otherwise we'll be too late for the coffee house! Have you seen that creature?"

"Yes, but will you get me a piece of bread and butter?"

Hilda has never gone hungry. Her father is a top-grade skilled worker. Her mother makes stockings, jerseys and warm gloves on a knitting machine. Hers is one of those rare working-class families in which gravy, bread, potatoes, lard and coffee are never absent from the table. And as the whole planetary system of domestic worries, conversations, desires and fears revolve around a warm *Stulle* (sandwich) spread thickly with firm white margarine, sacks of potatoes hidden under the bed, and food hanging up or stowed away in the box room, so too has Hilda's soul been formed from nice fat sausages oozing lard; when this soul grows up she will have the strong glossy crupper of a carthorse and the raw, nourishing smell of beer.

Hilda doesn't want to look at the ibis or any of the sceptical-looking long-feathered Egyptian birds that carry in outline, in every pleat of their grey plumage, the style and conventions of past millennia. The ibis struts up and down with the bald head and long nose of a wise old man wearing a cape but no trousers — so long and bare are its legs. Suddenly ecstasy and utter delight: "Look, look, it's got feathers on its tail like Aunt Wilhelmina's hat! Aunt Wilhelmina came round to see mummy this morning to get a free cup of coffee. People are getting so cheeky these days!"

A snowy night. By the Brandenburg Gate a snowy wind slices low across the asphalt like a sickle. The Tiergarten lies in deep shadow, looking like a dark wind-tossed sea. Parked by the empty pavements, as if alongside a quay, are lines of motor cars with their wet headlamps gleaming.

At half past five there is a Communist Party demonstration. Along Unter den Linden march the unemployed, musical instruments clanking in bags on their backs, cold inflamed ears sticking out from under caps, jacket collars turned up and wide bare gaps down their chests. The wind whistles in their faces. In the dark side-streets police rip down the little posters that for one day had plastered all Berlin. In the side-streets they hit out with rubber truncheons and break up the marches and then police officers are carried out of the crowd with fractured faces. On this blizzard-swept evening the ten thousand workers who flooded the Lustgarten and Unter den Linden as far as Friedrichstrasse greeted an armoured car with laughter whereas the police could not muster the courage to fire a single shot on the communist demonstration. That evening Hilda's mother is darning stockings under the lamp in the warm. Hilda is eating bread and lard and when she is quite full she rinses her satisfied tummy with water.

"Hilda," says mother, "sing the Internationale to us." Hilda sings the Internationale, then a song about a Christmas tree and then a favourite medley of psalms.

"Hilda," says her mother, "tell us how good children greet their uncle on his name-day." Aunt Wilhelmina, the wife of an unemployed worker, nods enviously and lavishes heated praise.

"Hilda," I ask, "what would you like for Christmas? A doll, a picture book or a real live camel like in the zoo?"

"Oh, uncle, give me some liver sausage!"

"Nonsense," Hilda's mother is saying to Aunt Wilhelmina, "I don't believe now in any sort of demonstration. We need an armed uprising, a real revolution, not those street processions out there."

The coffee pot sputters very quietly on the stove while the raging wind rattles the shutters behind the windows and howls like a demon.

"No," says Hilda's mother, tapping the white oil-cloth with her darning needle, "the eleventh hour has struck. You'll no longer lure us out into the streets whatever the ringing phrases. We need a decisive battle, not a demonstration. For five years all we've done has been to walk up and down!"

Aunt Wilhelmina is undecided:

"My old man has gone out. Good heavens, what a horrible winter night!"

"Come along to our silver wedding party, Wilhelmina! We'll be celebrating. There'll be cheese pie, meat pie, egg salad, cold potatoes and apples. And black pudding though I did have to sell the machine."

"Ooh, mummy, black pudding! Will I get some?"

"Everything's getting dearer and life's becoming impossible. All the same you are a bit to blame yourself, Wilhelmina. Everything depends upon the woman. If she is prudent, frugal and thrifty the home will never completely collapse. You should look after your things, they need perpetual care. Take that small crockery cupboard or the bed for example. They are both twenty-five years old. But could you tell? Not in the least. You need only wipe the dust off the shelves every morning, be careful how you treat the lacquered legs and not sit too often on the soft furniture."

"Mummy, Auntie Wilhelmina's son has just stolen a lump of sugar from our blue sugar bowl!"

"The main thing is to bear your misfortune bravely, don't let yourself go to pieces and never in any event sell your furnishings. As long as your things are intact the family will still hold out. What's more you shouldn't fall for the government's provocations. Until we have a decisive battle, no stupidities like these demonstrations. A bit more patience, endurance and solidarity. We have to support each other. Take Uncle Kurt for example. He'd been out of work for over a year of course and the whole family had to live in summer chalets out of town. His poor Minna had been ailing for two years until in the end she died of cancer. You can see from their example how in the end so much depends upon the woman. Her household fell totally apart. Absolutely everything went to rack and ruin. Well, naturally we relatives chipped in and arranged a proper, decent funeral for her. We workers have to help each other. I lent the poor old boy my husband's old top-hat. Well, at least he was able to walk behind the coffin dressed properly!"

Little Hilda is asleep on the corner of the bed, wearing a little white frock and white slippers and with a half-eaten piece of egg pie lying in her lap. This is pure enjoyment for Hilda: run round a bit, play a bit, eat her fill and then whistle blissfully through her little pink nose while the splendid pink bow on the top of her head quietly slips down on to Uncle Franz's shoulder. The silver wedding party went off really well. And what presents! Soap, margarine, flowers and two pounds of butter. The relatives clubbed together and presented them with six table sets and six teaspoons. The sewing-machine had had to be sold and the little boys smashed one of the vases with dry grasses that stood on the ledge under the mirror. But, for all that, the whole block knew that Hilda's mother was celebrating the twenty-fifth anniversary of her marriage really well and the whole street would be talking about it.

"The unions have folded up, of course. What do they still exist for, where do they get their funds from? From the boss, the industrialist. But we've outwitted our company, haven't we? And those gentlemen, they imagine that former trade union officials will really uphold their interests just for the couple of billion the management has doled out to them in their hardship."

Little Hilda's uncle gives a sly wink.

"Oh, no, you can't buy off those chaps! They may collect their salary from the capitalists but they are helping us, not them. We're closer to them: for heaven's sake, we've worked together for thirty years and we know each other. They'll win us those gold-based wages, don't you worry."

One of little Hilda's aunts is the widow of a communist killed last year. She could not give them anything so instead did the washing-up all evening at her wealthy relatives' home. She dries her hands that are red from the hot water and, taking her apron off, stands at the kitchen table to drink her glass of coffee and eat up the last two remaining sandwiches; then she asks her nephew, who leads the family band (guitar, violin and mandolin):

"Play me 'You fell a victim'."

In the back room the older folk had put out the light and by the reflection of a street light sung over and again the songs of their youth, in raucous unco-ordinated voices 'The Waltz of the Moon' and 'The Rose in the Glade'; now though there is just silence and the clink of coffee cups. But here, in the front room that is usually let to a lodger, the younger people press closely to each other, dancing their one-step to the speeded-up rhythm of the tragic funeral march of the revolution. Tiny Hilda is asleep. She is dreaming of margarine and Aunt Wilhelmina hiding a raisin-and-apple pie under her apron.

9 November in
a Working-Class District

The anniversary of the November revolution. A vast, half-empty, cavern-like hall. Several hundred unusually oppressed, taciturn and motionless workers — members of the Social-Democratic Party.

On the platform with a ghastly clarity, gold inscriptions on red linen. Much more like lines of verse — on the model of those pious proverbs that decorate tavern walls, greetings cards or a bridegroom's braces.

"Long live the International!" Which one is not said.

"Down with the Tyranny of Capital!"

"Liberty and Labour!"

No one looks, no one believes. Behind those stained holy banners, the red calico that mirrors the colour of fresh blood, and those inoffensive and innocuous excerpts from the Holy Scriptures, none of which has ever marched into battle at the head of the revolutionary proletariat, stand the five years of a vile and dissipated bourgeois republic that has shot down and sucked dry the workers of Germany under the cover of defused, emasculated revolutionary phrases.

The round, jauntily upturned lid of a beer-mug cannot be seen on a single table. Only here and there wisps of tobacco smoke melt into the damp grey cold. Workers have stopped drinking and

smoking long ago. A piece of dry bread pulled furtively out of the
pocket — that is enough to make the occasion.

They have come to this cheerless anniversary with their
wives and children. Looking like despondent emigrants sitting on a
quayside in the forlorn hope of a passage. The husbands are
chatting with their wives; the children, downcast and instinctively
bored, cuddle up to their mothers.

Meanwhile the fascists have planned their coup for that
very day, 9 November. Widespread demonstrations have been
proposed for the following morning with, possibly, street battles,
mass shootings of workers and pogroms — in short, a White coup.
This wretched November celebration may turn out to be the last
meeting between the rulers of the Social-Democratic Party and the
masses on which they lean for support and whose interests they are
pledged to defend — the last encounter between the governing
bureaucratic top brass and the proletariat against which the Whites
have promised to unleash their thugs within twenty-four hours.
But what did this 'workers' party' consider it necessary to tell
workers on the eve of the putsch? Did it give them arms? A worked
out plan of struggle? Assembly points, passwords, military and
political leadership? What would it have cost to organise
revolutionary defence in a city inundated with hundreds of
thousands of unemployed, an entire army of women thrown out on
to the streets, the disabled to whom the government pays a paltry
benefit and finally the droves of organised workers more than
twenty thousand of whom are already condemned to death by
starvation? Surely what else but a call for mobilisation and uprising
could possibly be issued at this meeting by the party that styles itself
a workers' and socialist party and has only just been kicked
ignominiously out of the government by a soldier's boot?

The assembled people awaited the party's representative
unusually agitated, and greeted him in absolute silence with the
unspoken question: just what shall we do now?

He had arrived: a refined party intellectual, a sceptic and a
sneerer, a member of the group that forms the left wing of the SPD
(not one right social democrat had plucked up the courage to address

any one of the numerous meetings that day). He spoke eloquently and at length for about two hours in all. What about? It is hard to recall. Not a word about the Whites at any rate. Not a sound about the coup planned for the next day. About the threat to the proletariat in such a coup, how to prevent it, how to organise defence, avoid provocations and a bloodbath — nothing. A smooth, clean-shaven parliamentary tract.

A few whining phrases about how the celebration had turned out not to be a cheerful one that day and that Germany had in fact no cause to rejoice on 9 November. Bread was getting dearer and unemployment growing, wicked generals were scheming against the republic and the peasants did not want to exchange their good harvest for fake slips of paper smeared with printing ink on one side only.

By now a completely funereal silence in the hall. Such cold hostility, despair and confusion gusted into the deputy's face that he decided to sprinkle the end of his speech with a few idealistic conclusions and then straight away disperse to its homes this demoralised proletariat that would in several hours' time have to encounter the Reichswehr's machine-guns, artillery and bayonets with its bare hands, without faith in itself nor even a right to such a faith.

Oh, what an ecstatic philosophical breeze that Doctor of Laws could all of a sudden waft through the cold, hungry vigilant meeting! A cheap, miserable yet seductive hope that can fool no one and never yet has defended anyone but none the less crawls into a proletarian heart like a louse on to the table only to be squashed by the iron fingernail of bourgeois dictatorship. And yet that traitor of a party rotting alive on the shoulders of the proletariat and poisoning it with its sugary ptomaine gets yet another chance to dodge the clear and simple fighting slogans of a break with the bourgeois government and for that hateful social revolution.

Just listen.

"We are beaten, unarmed, unemployed and robbed by our vile bourgeoisie. This celebration can rightly be called the funeral repast of the revolution. But, dear proletarians, don't get upset or angry: time, history and social destiny are on our side. The wheel of history cannot be turned back and therefore, in spite of our complete unreadiness for battle, the fascists will not triumph; go in peace and don't be afraid of Ludendorff. The guns are on his side but the logic of history is on ours. Good night and until we meet again — not on the barricades but at the next jubilee which, with the aid of social providence, will turn out happier than today's."

That's the lot.

Then a choir of at least fifty to sixty people sings sentimental songs for an hour and a half; on the stage a fine company of workers, divided into two lines by the flapping coat-tails of a socialist sexton, peer through their glasses at the nice clean sheets of music and with zeal and fervour sing exultations of pastoral bliss and pure love.

"O, swallow!" a fit-looking broad-shouldered building worker leads off, his solid Adam's apple sticking painfully out over the sweaty stand-up collar. His voice sounds as if his boots are too tight.

"O, those flowers of May!" a platoon of joiners and stevedores responds tenderly from the left-hand choir. Their tight jackets rustle over their magnificent bulging muscles. Not a stammer or a wrong note. Clearly the men have been practising ensemble performance for at least two months despite hunger, unemployment, the howling of unfed children and the fascists' preparations for war. No, nothing can divert the SPD from peaceful cultural and educational exercises.

To follow — a real madhouse. On to the stage they dragged the children of a whole working-class neighbourhood, a crowd of teenagers and a detachment of women and children. With the utmost thoroughness they gave themselves over to declaiming some sickeningly doleful play.

At a wave of the producer's baton hungry workers' children moan and weep before an audience of hungry workers:

"Mummy, bread!"

And then men, women and children together:

"Brothers, we are dy-ing!"

In the hall tears and hysterical sobs from the women.

The crowd disperses in a weakened, irritated and helpless

mood. Its healthy anger and enormous discontent, the arsenal of revolution, have been flushed down the sewer of a debilitating and depraved pseudo-art. Cunning those SPDers! Towards the end the very same choir that had heroically managed top C performs, among other lyrical songs, the Internationale. This is to foster the impression in the proletariat that this music is not indissolubly linked to revolutionary action and that its drums do not have to sound out only amid blood and powder-smoke.

No, that dangerous battle-cry must be tamed in advance and cooped up into the general hen-run of songs so that on the day of war, before the assault, it will not stir the proletarian's ear nor unfurl over his head like a fresh banner flapping in the wind.

Another SPD meeting. Hertz, a Reichstag member, attempts to speak. The workers prevent him as far as they can. On the side of the Reichstag member: the chairman's bell, statistics, history, political economy and logic. On the side of the workers: piercing catcalls, unemployment, hunger and a healthy social instinct. Hertz considers that over the last five years the SPD has made certain mistakes but that they are not worth talking about now. The audience on the other hand wishes to talk about nothing but these mistakes and dozens of notes sent up to Dr Hertz put it in black and white: "The SPD is a stinking corpse which it is high time to bury." When the Reichstag member shows by his look that he cannot read out what has been written down it is repeated to him aloud.

The platform do not want to give a communist the right to answer.

The workers vote solidly for him and the communist speaks for forty minutes with the chairman's permission and for another forty despite his ruling against. Then deputy Hertz surfacing somehow through the noise, stamping and heckling, makes a frantic effort, suddenly takes a grip, and is triumphantly afloat.

He has found allies and names names that turn the workers into pillars of salt.

"Any resistance to the Whites is useless. (Whistling). For

the five years that Social Democracy has sat down with them in the government it has attempted to uphold the interests of workers. (The noise rises.) Social Democracy did what it could but the Black Hundred ministers pressured Stresemann and Ebert so much that these unfortunate comrades could hardly refuse a huge monthly subsidy to Kahr's White Guard government in Bavaria. (Abuse for the speaker.) Lenin . . . (A deep silence; Hertz can take a breath). Lenin proved that Germany does not exist as a self-sufficient political and economic entity. Her fate is linked with the revolution or reaction in France, Belgium, Britain and Italy. Basing ourselves upon Lenin's view we can safely state that the possibility of social revolution in Germany at the present moment is absolutely excluded . . ."

Dr Hertz is seen to be still speaking for his mouth is moving. But his words can no longer be heard.

Hamburg at the Barricades

Hamburg

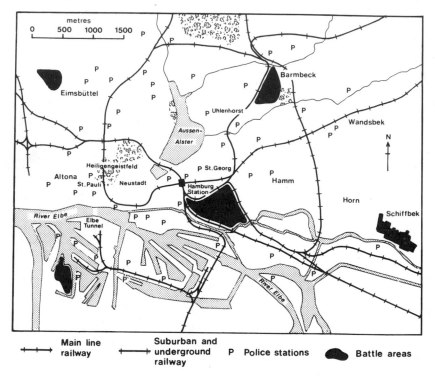

Main line railway · Suburban and underground railway · P Police stations · Battle areas

An uprising passes by without trace in big cities. A revolution has to be great and victorious if the traces of havoc, its heroic abrasions and white bullet-scars on walls pock-marked by machine-gun fire are to be preserved on stone and iron if only for a few years.

Two or three days or two or three weeks later, together with shreds of newspapers and tattered posters either ripped from the walls by bayonet points or washed off by dirty showers of rain, the brief memory of street battles, churned-up roadways and trees thrown like bridges across river-like streets and stream-like alleyways also passes away.

Prison doors slam behind the convicted while fellow-fighters, thrown out of their factories, are compelled to look for work in another city or a remote district; those who are unemployed following the defeat take refuge in the most far-flung and anonymous nooks; the women keep quiet, the children, wary of the security policeman's smarmy inquiries, deny everything. Thus the legend of the days of the Rising dies away, forgotten and drowned by the noise of restored traffic and resumed work. In corners of workshops a new group of workers that has taken over at the deserted benches in the factories may still repeat a name or two and recall the particularly good shots — but that too is passing away.

For a worker there is no history within the confines of the bourgeois state; the list of his heroes is kept by the drumhead court-martial and the factory guard from a Menshevik* trade union. The bourgeoisie, once having cracked down with armed force, stifles the hateful memory of the danger it has so recently escaped.

Several months have already passed since the Hamburg Rising. But, strange as it may seem, its memory stubbornly refuses to vanish: yet the traces of barricades have been carefully smoothed over, trains run peacefully along the embankments and viaducts that served as defensive or offensive parapets and seagulls rest on them.

Three drumhead sausage-machines hastily shove the street fighters into jail; the doctors and prison inspectors have long ago re-

---

* 'Menshevik' is used in *Hamburg at the Barricades* in a general colloquial sense of 'right-wing-dominated' or 'reformist'. (R.C.)

turned to the next of kin the last corpses mutilated beyond recognition by brutality. And still the memory of that daring October endures. There is not a public house, workers' gathering or proletarian family in the old free city of Hamburg in which the amazing scenes enacted on those outlying streets are not recounted with the pride of a participant or at least the involuntary admiration of an onlooker.

The explanation for the obstinacy with which the dockland proletariat maintains and watches over the memory of the October days lies in the fact that the Hamburg Rising was not smashed in a military, political or moral sense. The masses were not left with the deep gall of defeat.

The protracted revolutionary process that had impelled them to the barricades in October was broken neither on the 24th when the whole police force and a crack Black Hundred unit of marines and Reichswehr forces were mobilised, nor on the 26th when compact police formations, thousands-strong cavalry and infantry detachments and whole platoons of armoured cars finally burst into the revolutionary suburbs which several hours before had been voluntarily abandoned by the workers' hundreds. On the contrary, the movement that surfaced in October to rule the city for sixty hours, cracking the enemy's head everywhere he dared to launch an assault upon the skilfully placed barricades, cost the workers only ten dead but the police and troops dozens and hundreds of dead and wounded and afterwards calmly led its combatants out of the fire, saved and hid their weapons, brought its wounded into secure refuges in a planned retreat and then returned underground so as to be able to re-emerge at the first call of the all-German revolution.

The beginning of the revolutionary movement has to be counted not from October but from August of last year when Hamburg had become the arena of successive bitter wage battles, for an eight-hour day, pay based on the gold equivalent and a whole range of not only economic but also purely political demands: a workers' government, control of production and so forth. These trade union battles were accompanied by a rising strike fever and stormy outbursts of growing revolutionary hatred: raids on food warehouses and assaults on police and blacklegs. It was during these months especially that Hamburg working women distinguished themselves, being, like all women from large ports, far more resourceful and politically mature than their comrades in the majority of Germany's industrial centres. In the August of that year it was they who barred their husbands' and workmates' way into the striking shipyards. Neither police bayonets nor the weak-willed crowds of workers who were ready to meet their employers on any conditions could thrust their human chain back from the Elbe tunnel. One of these clashes ended with the disarming and beating up of a police detachment and, in particular, of the lieutenant who led it: for this he was drowned in the cold dirty waters of the Elbe.

This movement starting in August could not have ended in fiasco as the bourgeoisie crowed. Nor could it have fallen with the brilliant military demonstration of 23-26 October but only with the defeat or victory of the whole German working class. In this continuity and in this constant and protracted growth which marks the work of the Hamburg comrades lies the crucial distinction between an armed uprising and the so-called political 'putsch'.

A 'putsch' has neither past nor future; only total victory or an equally irrevocable and futile defeat. A revolution, if it is to be powerful and guided by a strong and elastic battle-ready party, must be able to spring itself, pull back and recoil even after the most reckless sally. But a weak, politically untrained and untempered proletariat will live only in the hope of a brief blow, an outburst and very sharp, bloody but unsustained effort. Such a brief blow may well cost enormous sacrifices and the utmost effort but fragile and loosely-knit masses will face anything provided that beyond that momentary assault there glimmers some hope of an ephemeral but incontestably complete and final success. If after such an attempt at seizing power there follows a setback for one reason or another these masses will fall out of line, drop out of any organisation and reinforce their defeat with acrimonious self-criticism. Regular cadres of politically mature masses will, on the other hand, return from a storming operation to their old entrenchments still equal to long, gruelling, slow siege, sapper work in the underground and daily harrying operations. The Hamburg Rising, by virtue of the prolonged political process leading up to it and even more by the absolutely brilliant work carried out in the days and weeks immediately following its liquidation, forms the classic example of a truly revolutionary uprising, evolving a quite remarkable strategy of street battles and a faultless retreat, unique of its kind, that left the masses with a sure sense of superiority over the enemy and an awareness of moral victory.

Its results are unquestionable: never before has the collapse of the old trade union organisations reached such elemental proportions as it did after those very October days. From 25 October to 1 January more than thirty thousand members, each of many years' standing, dropped out of the ranks of the Menshevik trade unions. We shall go into detail below on the dastardly role played by the trade union bureaucracy and its right wing during the October days. The United Republicans and the Fatherland Defence Leagues, acting as a Menshevik household guard, publicly relieved the police in the quietest districts, thereby allowing the latter to concentrate on subduing Hamm and Schiffbek. More about that below — here we shall just note that all these bellicose exploits by social democracy led to party cards being torn up and dumped in heaps at the doors of its recruiting offices.

They lay in piles on the doorstep and hundreds of workers, risking arrest or being shot by Reichswehr patrols, made their way to the trades union hall to toss their card at the treachery-besmirched face of the bureaucracy. A whole number of the major trade unions in the coastal region such as, for example, the Amalgamated Union of Building Workers, came apart at every seam after the October Rising. It was physically impossible to restrain members from a demonstrative mass exodus from the union. I managed to attend the meeting of one of the builders' branches that had, eight-hundred-strong, decided to leave the union and organise its own association. Among those present were middle-aged men, not all party members, masters of their trade and not short of employment, men who had paid their dues for decades.

At such a meeting old men choking with fury demanded a complete and immediate break with the 'bonzes'. No communist could have more strongly hated or more deeply sensed the immeasurable decline of the old party. Communist Party (KPD) members endeavoured in vain to dissuade the meeting from forming a 'breakaway union' and to insist on undermining the bureaucracy from the inside by forming a solid opposition that could increasingly extend its influence . . .

Workers disown the union as something utterly filthy and unworthy of a single hard-earned penny contributed to its funds. They have become deeply convinced that a worker who remains in a Menshevik union for as much as a day forfeits his proletarian honour and becomes party to the falsehood, murders and betrayal of the SPD. After October, staying in the union, even for a middle-aged non-party worker became tantamount to service with the *Sipo** or the *Eins A*†.

The Communist Party and the masses behind it have grown infinitely stronger, externally as well as internally. Their activity has not abated in spite of numerous arrests (incidentally the majority of comrades were seized not during the Rising itself but only when it was over and on the basis of voluntary denunciations made by SPD workers and neighbours). On the contrary all the walls of Hamburg are decorated with ineffaceable inscriptions. At every crossroads and on the corner of every public building the inscription is invariably painted up: 'The Communist Party lives. It cannot be banned.'

Parliament may well vote for an *Ermächtgungsgesetz* (Enabling Act); Seeckt may well enjoy special powers and a White dictatorship may well gulp down the last dregs of tiny freedoms in labour legislation, yet the walls of all the huts where the unemployed register are pasted over with new little communist posters like wallpaper. They are sprinkled like snow from the gallery at all SPD meetings, stuck on pub walls and tram and underground train windows. The women of the outlying areas, where all the male population is on the run or in various prisons, demand that posters and

---

* *Sicherzeitspolizei* — security police. (R.C.)

† Unit A, the plain-clothes branch of the security police. (R.C.)

leaflets be sent out and if they have one grievance it is the lack of a cheap communist newspaper. All this so little resembles a defeat that the drumhead court-martial judges, under pressure from the masses' silent threat, try to mitigate the sentences. The convicted go to the fortress or hard labour camp with the pride and tranquillity of victors, in the unassailable certainty that the revolution will never allow their five, seven or ten years of solitary confinement to run their course, and with the most profound scornful disdain for the laws of the bourgeois state, the cowardly brutality of its police force and the seemingly triumphant weight of its prison walls. Such a faith cannot mislead.

So why didn't the whole country support the Hamburg Rising?

In the October days the whole of Germany was divided into two camps confronting each other and awaiting the signal for the offensive. But by then Saxony had already been inundated by the police and the Reichswehr. Thus by the time of the Hamburg Rising one of the revolution's principal bridgeheads had in effect ceased to exist. Numerous groups of unemployed still filled Dresden's nighttime streets but hard on their heels, alongside and ahead of them, Reichswehr units, armed, insolent and provocative, bit into the asphalt. A signal for battle given in Saxony at this moment would probably have become the signal for the mass slaughter of Saxon workers. During these very days a conference at Hamburg of workers employed in the great shipyards of Hamburg, Lübeck, Stettin, Bremen and Wilhelmshaven was demanding the immediate declaration of a general strike and the leaders only just managed to obtain from this policy-making conference a postponement of the strike for a few days — yet the workers' conference at Chemnitz turned down a general strike. By now Saxony was under water and the proletariat, devoted to the left social democrats to the last, turned instinctively away from an unfavourable collision that could perhaps have been fatal to the revolution.

Berlin! Anyone who has seen Berlin in the October days will certainly recall a feeling of astonishing ambivalence or, rather, ambiguity as the basic feature of its revolutionary turmoil. Women and unemployed gave the streets a special tint. In the bread queues and in front of butchers' windows smart urchins whistling the Internationale pushed through between knots of despairing women. The slide of the mark, the derisory benefits paid out to the unemployed, disabled and war widows, the inflated rates of pay, the breath-taking prices of immediate necessities, the ruination of the petty-bourgeoisie, the utter shamelessness of the Grand Coalition, the cupping-glass that the Ruhr had become, the repressions by the French, the quiet mischiefs done by German capitalists that had been dragged into the light of day by the press and, overshadowing all the newspaper columns, the spectre of the bloodied and coal-dust-covered Ruhr — all these were the clear portents of a revolution at hand. Rich people's motor cars were already avoiding the suburbs and the police turned a blind eye to the looting of bakers' shops. On the outskirts artillery kept rumbling over the stony wastes, edging ever closer to the striking factories; the roar of lorries loaded with two tidily-formed lines of police did not moderate, but merely went to kindle the fury of the crowd besieging the markets and newspaper kiosk windows.

Yet at the same time, vast and totally passive masses of workers still subscribed to social democracy; hidden behind the backs of the unemployed and communists were the extensive layers of the bourgeoisified proletariat, greedily clutching at a piece of bread, domestic comfort and a pound of margarine, however many hours it might be needed to earn all that. A cowardly, shrill, disgruntled majority ready to sit out two or three days at home by the fire behind a cup of lenten coffee and the latest little sheet of *Vorwärts* until the shooting in the street dies down, the dead and wounded are carried away, the barricades dismantled and the victor, whoever he may be — a Bolshevik, Ludendorff or Seeckt — has put the vanquished in jail and a lawful government in the seat of power. Alongside an extremely active vanguard there was this distended, decayed, expectant rear ready in event of a failure to denounce a communist neighbour who had lain in a trench beneath the very window of some worthy socialist official concealed behind his net curtain.

In Berlin as in Hamburg (only certain quarters with a sol-idly working-class population excepted) the proletariat had to res-ist General Seeckt's gendarmerie and troops in complete isolation without the active assistance of broad masses, without hope of rein-forcements at the toughest moments and sometimes, as in Ham-burg, with virtually no weapons. Nevertheless the rising in Ham-burg undertaken in equally, or almost equally unfavourable condi-tions, not only did not lead to defeat but gave quite astounding re-sults. The truth is that behind it stood the whole of working-class Germany that, *unbroken by the counter-revolution in an open bat-tle,* could materially and morally cover the heroic retreat of the Hamburg pioneers.

Anyway, the job of a party out to conquer is not just to keep a feverish watch out for the historic moment, that so-called 'twelfth hour of the bourgeoisie', when the hands of the clock of history hesi-tate for an instant and then mechanically count off the first seconds of the communist era.

There is an old German tale: a valiant knight spent all his life in a magic cave waiting for a slowly swelling drip of water glis-tening from the tip of a stalactite to drop finally into his mouth. At the last minute some absurdity would always stop him from catch-ing the agonisingly awaited drip which would fall uselessly on the sand. The worst part of course is not the actual point of failure but the dead, hollow pause of disillusioned expectation between one burst and the next.

In Hamburg they did not wait for dew from heaven. What they here so neatly and tersely call *Die Aktion* was linked into a strong chain of uninterrupted struggle, knitted to what had gone be-fore and finding its support in a future every day of which, be it one of success or failure, stands under the sign of a victory that will smash the world like the head of a steam-hammer.

Besides, the Rising occurred not in the province of Branden-burg, not in Prussia, and not in the Berlin of parliament, the Siegsal-lee and Seeckt, but on the *Wasserkante,* in English, the seaside.

Hamburg

Hamburg lies on the shore of the North Sea like a big wet fish lifted still quivering from the water.

Eternal fogs settle down on the pointed scaly roofs of its houses. Not one day remains true to its capricious, pale, windy morning. With the tide's ebb and flow there follow in succession damp, mildness, sunshine, the grey cold of the open sea and the interminable relentless rain that drenches the glistening asphalt like someone standing on the foreshore picking up from the sea an old ship's bucket — the kind used for baling out leaky boats that choke with water in a heavy swell — and swilling it out over gay Hamburg; Hamburg, as impermeable as a pilot's oilskins, steaming with moisture, reeking like a seaman's pipe, charred with the fires of the dockside bars yet standing firm under the torrential rain with legs set wide apart as if on deck, planted on the right and left banks of the Elbe.

All along the shores of this marvellous industrial inlet, nature has been universally eradicated like some prejudice left out of our life by the eighteenth century. Not an inch of ground left bare. Over a stretch of twenty or so miles are two trees, more resembling masts after a fire at sea than the useless living things they are: the one on the jetty is hunched up like an old woman walking against the wind on to whose thick woollen stockings and shivering legs the wind tosses shreds of angry foam; the other is at the offices of Hamburg's greatest shipyards, Blohm & Voss.

This one only stays up out of fear; beneath it is a disgusting black canal into which factory waste flows from gaping pipes like inky vomit. A bridge, the guard's cabin and, on the opposite bank in the pale light of five o' clock in the morning, nothing but the shining windows of invisible blocks without walls or roofs in row after row up above the whole harbour, reaching out with their electricity to touch the very dawn.

But the greatest of all these wonders, and the shapeliest forms in this realm of shapely metal, are the light shadowy jibs of the world's largest cranes that arch over the harbour. Lying at their feet like toys are transatlantic liners, fully fitted-out with their illuminated rows of portholes and hideous parts below the water-line, like swans out of water which have equally ugly underwater parts.

Here they are working three shifts, convulsively and ruth-lessly.

Here, by wringing out the workers like wet washing, the German bourgeoisie is making its last futile attempts to surmount the crisis that paralyses it: building, creating new values and popu-lating the oceans with its black-funnelled white ships from whose sterns flutter the old imperial black-white-red banners with scarcely noticeable republican pock-marks on one of their fields.

As they say, Hamburg has everything — the smoke of fac-tory chimneys, the elephant-trunks of the cranes with which the iron mammoths ravage the holds and fill up the stone depositories, the light, gently sloping bridges criss-crossing the new-born ships, wet beds, the howl of the sirens, the coarse yells of the hooters, the ebb and flow of the ocean that makes sport with the jetsam and the seagulls that settle on the water like floats, and the neat cubical dark red brick masses of the warehouses, offices, plants, markets and customs houses all built in straight lines and looking like oblong piles of cargo recently stacked by the dockers.

Armies and legions of workers are employed in these ship-yards, on loading and unloading the ships, in the innumerable engineering, oil-refining and chemical plants, the several large-scale manufacturing works and the vast industrial installations that cover Hamburg's rear, that marshy, sandy hinterland, with an un-broken crust of concrete and steel.

The Elbe, this ancient, dirty, warm-watered coaching-yard for sea tramps, is continually extending and building on to its con-creted backyards.

Here the sea horses throw down their baggage, gulp down oil and coal and get cleaned and washed while their captains give in their bribes at the customs, touch up the bills and have a shave be-fore going ashore to their families; meanwhile the crews go off and get nabbed *en masse* in St. Pauli, a quarter for bars, gangs, ready-made dresses, pawnshops where the same garish, shoddily-made ex-pensive dress can be lodged for half its price and finally the most as-tounding brothels. Ever since medieval times the back streets of the St. Pauli neighbourhood have been screened off from the city by strong iron gates open only at night. They are finely wrought with every conceivable device and whimsical detail, proudly decorated with the emblems and insignia of the craft's guild. In the evenings a lighted window opens up in every door that gives on to a back street and there, on display, smiling into the endless rainy darkness, are the queens of these seamen's paradises. They wear low-cut dresses, drawn in at the waist and trimmed with spangles and feathers, dresses in which the fashions from the end of the last century have survived to the present, as on sweet-wrappers and in the imagination of woman-starved seamen, and have always been thought to embody the supreme joy of living.

This line of living meat is sold with the utmost simplicity. Customers pass from window to window, examine the goods on dis-play and disappear inside only to fly out into the road a short while later growling and cursing: St. Pauli's doorkeepers are renowned for their muscle.

All languages echo and all nations mingle in the little tav-erns of this district. They are famed for their savage wit, egg grog and a total immunity from police intervention — in short, a won-derful blend of valour, alcohol, revolutionary ardour, tobacco smoke and the latest hopelessly fallen, wilted sinner; she balances on the edge of a table swamped in bitter beer hastily repeating over a piece of bread and butter to some drunken Adam without name or face that most divine lie — about love.

The language spoken here is, as a rule, Hamburg's language.

It is thoroughly soaked in the sea; as salty as cod; as round and juicy as a Dutch cheese; as rough, pungent and jolly as English gin; as slithery, rich and light as the scales of some large rare deep-sea fish slowly panting among the carps and plump eels quivering their wet rainbows in a fishwife's basket. Only the letter S, sharp as a spindle and as graceful as a mast, testifies to Hamburg's old gothic and the days of the Hanse and the piracy of the archbishops.

Not only the lumpen-proletariat but the whole city is steeped in the lively, boisterous spirit of the port. It surrounds on all sides in a tight ring the bourgeois quarters situated around the Alster, a tidal lake in which the pulse of that same Baltic ebb and flow can still be felt. Villas hug the shore closely, leaving barely enough space to run through the neat gardens clad in flowers like swimming costumes, and tennis courts down the flight of steps to the shore.

Everywhere the excited, unclean breath of the suburbs blows down the necks of the patricians' houses. A ring of electric trains firmly binds in the outskirts and squeezes them against the smart quarters like a steel band; along it, filling the coaches with the smell of sweat, tar and winey breath, a turbid stream of workers surges twice daily, bisecting the whole city on its way to the docks.

Consequently all of Hamburg is equally attentive to the lunchtime hooter at the shipyards, the boatswain's whistle and the morning and evening call-over on the bank of the Elbe just as the smallest pool and the tiniest child-packed frog pond heeds the shudders of the distant ocean, the ocean that sends Hamburg its wealth and its winds that are as resilient as sails.

The bourgeois, the worthy burgher, is just as uninsured against contact and proximity with the proletarians as is his home. A lady going to the theatre is squashed between two portworkers who quite naturally put their greasy bags down on the soft seats.

A young thing from St. Pauli sits herself coolly down beside a civil servant's wife, winks round at her neighbours and gets off at her stop on the arm of one of them; a worker cuddles his wife or girl-friend; a stevedore smokes out those around him with an incredible tobacco, some friends take a seaman home from a binge and the whole coach chuckles with them, thinking, speaking and laughing in the purest Hamburg *Platt* (dialect) that can turn any place into a jolly seaman's fo'c's'le.

All this is not very consequential from our point of view. But after Berlin where a worker with his tools has the right to travel only in a specially dirty old coach; where the superiority of the first and second classes is all but defended by the police; where an unemployed worker, rubbing his cold violet ears dares not seat himself on one of the Tiergarten's innumerable and always vacant benches; after exultant bourgeois Berlin, the very air of Hamburg with its free and natural spirit smells of revolution..

At four or five o' clock in the morning the lumpen-proletar-iat is asleep, wherever that might be, or is being forwarded on to the police station.

At a quarter to six, still by the light of electricity, the first high tide of workers begins.

Above the tramlines a railway hangs in the darkness and above that the short gleaming ribbons of the electric trains: all these thrust on to the pavement an army of dockers, hundreds of thousands of workers and hundreds and thousands more unem-ployed who besiege the wharves in hope of some casual employ-ment. Each unit gathers around its foreman; in the blackness of tarry jackets and from behind backs humped with tool-bags there shines an oil-lamp like a colliery overman's. After the call-over the regiments of workers split up for the hundreds of steamboats that distribute them around the yards and plants. They pour into the in-dustrial city over four bridges. Troops and police keep a sharp eye to see that not one 'civvie' penetrates the industrial islands. But neither the bridges nor the hundreds of steamers that play their lamps and searchlights upon the river in a sort of unique carnival in a black oily Venice, suffice for the dense surge of the morning shift. A bright dry tube that pumps legions of workers across from shore to shore every morning and evening, has been laid deep beneath the Elbe's waters.

At each end of the tunnel elephantine lifts raise and lower this human torrent to and from the concrete exits.

They move, these two lifts, screeching in their screw-like towers like two shovels unceasingly stoking living fuel into hundreds of furnace-like factories. Out of this forge came the Hamburg Rising.

Barmbeck

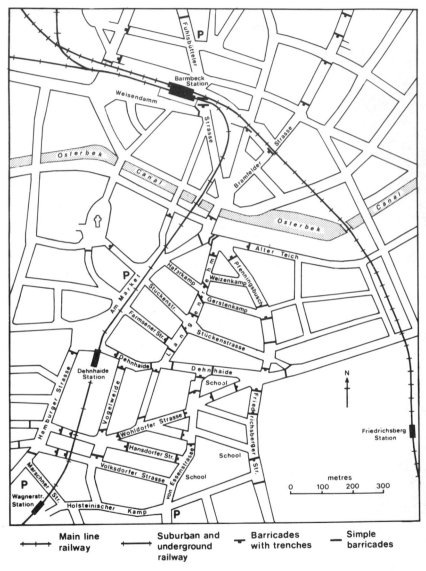

┼┼┼ **Main line railway**	┼ **Suburban and underground railway**
┳ **Barricades with trenches**	▬ **Simple barricades**

P Police stations

Barmbeck

Hamburg workers live a long way from their factories and shipyards, in a part of the city christened Barmbeck. This is one enormous barracks for workers where all the dwellings look like one another, common sleeping quarters in rented barracks joined together by the unclean, bare, damp corridors of the streets. Opening up at the ends of these streets like chinks are dreary squares that look more like public kitchens or conveniences, each with a dreary fountain under the tin sky. Across this already foul and filthy suburb crawls the gigantic caterpillar of the railway viaduct describing a steel semi-circle. Its slightly bowed legs cling to the asphalt with concrete suckers. A rattlesnake's head tightly fitting between two blocks, vanishes amid the backyard crevices, blind walls and ravines crammed with bunches of giddy little balconies from which flutter drying linen and strands of wilting ivy that has had its fill of smoke and damp. The station building plants a wide, flat foot on the railway line's tail, leaving a crack for the stream of passengers to pour through.

Directly opposite the station, behind a spiked railing from which shreds of old decrees dangle, stands one of the police stations with murky windows that resemble a detective's shaded glasses. A guard on duty, that pock-marked monotony of police stations and the official's tedious boredom and spite, chewed over like an already twice smoked and discarded cigarette-end picked up from the floor.

The port is open to workers only at certain times. It sucks in an army of workers at dawn and spits every one of them out in the evening. Troops remain in this deserted industrial fortress to guard the swing-bridges, turnstiles, and subways through which the dense flood of workers pours to the quayside. Not one worker lives within the port itself. Only the old and proven servants of the *seigneurs* of industry enjoy such a privilege; the sparse, obsequiously twinkling lights of their dwellings huddle timidly against the gigantic shadows of factory blocks slowly exhaling into the night and fog the human warmth they have swallowed up during the day. The guards pace up and down the quays using their bayonets to block the way of any stranger they want to check on and shining their lamps straight into his face:

"Who are you? Where're you going? Why? Password."

In Barmbeck the unrest began a week before the Rising. On Wednesday 17 October working women and office workers' wives take over the markets and force the saboteur traders to continue business.

On Thursday and Friday they form a chain in front of the shipyards and send their shamed husbands back home. On the same day fifteen thousand unemployed workers and women demonstrate at the Heiligengeist Field. On Saturday an impressive rally at the Trade Union House from which thousands proceed to the City Hall and break through into the restricted zone surrounding it.

On the streets that evening tens of thousands of workers pace endlessly, stubbornly, intently and furiously along the pavements. The police arrest over a hundred people but the sombre promenades do not cease. News of the Reichswehr's onslaught upon the workers of Saxony spreads like a fever. The masses are gripped by a terrible excitement. This is the eve of revolution.

On Sunday 21 October there is a conference of portworkers from the whole Baltic coast: from Bremen, Stettin, Schweinemunde, Lübeck and Hamburg. The majority of delegates are SPD but many have been sent from plants already several days on strike. They had already returned their membership cards to the metalworkers' union which had declared these strikes to be 'wild-cat'. There was a sharp clash between an old *SPD-Mann,* a Stettin delegate, a man covered in moss and mould from twenty-eight years of social-officialdom, and T. a square, big-boned, wide-browed worker who would pound his clenched fist like a shaft and was to grasp the reins of the Hamburg Rising in his iron hands.

Here, at this conference, T. had to urge on and restrain simultaneously. Like some old coachman, used to driving his heavily laden waggons up the steep icy slopes of the bridges, T. had both to kindle and damp down, scarcely keeping on his box while beating off the social-bureaucrats with piercing whipcracks, tugging on the foaming bits with the whole weight of his authority and grounding the rearing militancy that would argue no longer but was blind with rage.

The conference only just permitted the postponement of a general strike for several days. Only thanks to this resolution could a stormy meeting of full-time officials be convinced and brought to order.

On Sunday night a courier brings (false) news of an eruption in Saxony. The order for a general strike is immediately passed round the various quarters. Dozens of major enterprises support the Deutschewerft shipyards which have been locked out since Saturday.

The second shift of workers leaves the workshops, breaks through the police cordons and goes back to the city centre. By four o'clock the harbour is paralysed. A crowd, one-hundred thousand-strong, roams the streets of Hamburg giving it the look of a city already in the grip of the Rising.

A second courier: he speaks at meetings in Altona and Neustadt giving entirely fantastic news of the Russian Army mobilising and their submarines sailing to the aid of Hamburg.

In the dead of night a conference of the 'chiefs': the leaders of the Military Organisation receive their combat orders, taking them with a feeling of the deepest inner satisfaction. T., who has been fighting for a postponement for several hours, stopping up all the holes through which the movement might have spilled prematurely on to the streets, now lifts all the sluices and opens all the taps that still hold back the torrent of the Rising.

K. also was pleased. A few words about him.

A worker. A sergeant-major in the war who loathed with all his being what is called *der preussische Drill* (Prussian army drill) in the trenches. He had received a commission for his bravery. Then, in one of the towns of occupied Galicia a major incident that nearly cost him his nice new epaulettes. Four weeks' jail for boxing a major's ears in public. By 1918 K. is a member of the Hamburg Council of Workers' Deputies. He takes part in the March Action. He had already, just after the Unification Congress, joined the KPD. One of the most active members of the Hamburg organisation. Taken all together, military training, courage, roughness, a portworkers' jollity, the old sergeant-major's precise abrupt speed and the knack of 'delivering a rocket', all these unexcelled qualities won K. popularity among the masses and a cautious, almost squeamish reaction from *die Intellektuellen*. And well they might for philistines don't like grinning people with an invariable smell of *Köm* (Kümmel spirits) about them and the markedly crude language of the port.

Gaiety, roughness and a slight intoxication in the blood are considered incompatible with the calling of a European party hack.

After the August riots the party was literally deluged with spies. One of them, with the touch of an old provocateur, offered to supply a crate of arms, receipt of which would have led to the dismemberment of the military organisation. K. was charged with unmasking this police ruse. He drove off with the agent to collect the arms. On one of the bridges he coolly picked the man up by the scruff of the neck and dangled him over the side.

"Own up, you bastard."

He owned up, got his due and vanished.

In periods of lull comrade K.'s wild energy turns him into a pub brawler and tyrant, terror and pride of a whole neighbourhood.

He meets a bunch of SPD men in a pub: Hamburg's superb *Köm* mixed half-and-half with the excellent beer sharpens K.'s dialectic to the extreme. In the end the Mensheviks, aroused to a fury by the silent taunts of this giant with the narrowed, benign, crafty eyes, leap yelling into a fight. Taking the ringleader as his target K. snatches him from amongst his fellow-thinkers and flings him on to a grand piano. An incident, the police, broken noses and unimaginable chords from the unfortunate instrument. Inactivity is terribly dangerous for people like K. Yet in an active struggle they move forward into the front ranks.

During the Rising it was that same K. and the communist officer Kb. who saved Barmbeck from rout by a network of amazing barricades. More about them below.

At midnight the leaders disperse to brief and assemble the members of the workers' hundreds. The party as a whole was, like the wide layers of workers not in the party, only to learn of the Rising during the morning after the seizure of all police stations by the military organisation's commandos. The storming of the *Polizeibüros* was scheduled for dawn on 23 October, i.e. simultaneously in all parts of the city at 4.45 a.m. and, immediately following the take-over of the police stations, the capture and disarming of Wandsbek barracks. Until that point the military leaders, who had mobilised their men and had to spend the rest of the night with them, could not allow anyone to go home, put a light on or on any pretext go off to 'say good-bye to the family'. Only thanks to such precautions were the police caught truly off-guard and disarmed with bare hands. The credit must go to T. and the other comrades who worked out this battle plan with him. The game was half won by prefacing the mass Rising with this silent unexpected blow by the military organisation which: 1) deprived the enemy of support points in the form of police stations; 2) armed the workers at the expense of the police; and 3) produced in the masses an awareness of victory already ensured, thereby attracting them more easily to join a struggle that had hardly begun. The government paid tribute to this dislocation caused by the Rising. Here is what Hamburg *Polizeisenator* (Police Commissioner) Hense, a social democrat, wrote about it:

"The worst thing about this Rising was by no means the numerical weakness nor the inadequacy of the forces placed at our disposal. No, what was so terrible *(schreklich)* was that this time, unlike all previous putsches, the communists were able to carry though their lengthy and thorough preparations in such secrecy that not a single squeak about it reached us. Generally we tend to be informed of everything afoot in the communists' camp. Not that we have to keep special spies in their ranks. No, *the law-abiding public, in which I include workers who are members of the Social-Democratic Party,* usually keeps us informed about everything happening amongst the communists without any coercion.'

This time the 'law-abiding' Mensheviks proved unable to forewarn the authorities about the Rising in preparation. The latter knew nothing of it, so little in fact that the state of siege that had kept the police on full alert the week before had been lifted by the government on Sunday, that is on the eve of the Rising.

But let us go back a few hours. Here are some trivialities that portray the mood of the party at the moment of mobilisation, the time when people are caught unawares, promptly shaken out of bed and led off by the scruff of the neck to goodness knows where. This is the twilight hour when, lying half-awake getting unbearably cold, you want to go back to sleep and everything is painted in a drab muddy colour — in short not quite the time when you get up to adopt a heroic posture. Everything is, as they say, rough and ready.

One of the leaders of the Rising goes round his *Bezirkslei-ter* (zone leaders) to pass on the order for the morning's operation.

A street without life, a sleeping house, a somnolent, stuffy, snoring flat. The family of a very poor worker. He rose and dressed without asking why or lingering a minute. A calm handshake and a cigarette's slowly receding ember in the dark.

Another nook — in one of the working-class quarters. The door is opened by the wife who helps her husband collect his things and holds a candle-stub over the kitchen table on which a map is spread out. For some time he primes himself and then, from the depths of his heart with a sense of the deepest relief:

"Endlich geht's los . . ." (At last it's beginning.)

In a third lair a wife to her husband who is dawdling over getting ready:

"Nu mock di man fertig" (Hurry up and get ready.)

Finally the St. Georg district. Here they're not asleep. In a back room a lamp is alight, flicking the web of tobacco smoke. The landlady answers evasively — he's at home and he isn't and she doesn't know anything. Cautious steps on the stairs and suddenly comrade R. appears in the doorway, his face smeared with soot, barefoot, with a cluster of rifles under his arm, his pockets stuffed with all sorts of ammunition. In shadow is the merrily grinning physiognomy of a character known around the dockland taverns as *Rowdy* (ruffian). What's this? They have cleared out a whole armoury. This *Genosse* (comrade) is of course not quite a *Genosse*, only a sympathiser. But the speed and dexterity with which he unhooked the bolt and lifted the shop window . . . *Rowdy* prides himself on the simplicity of the great performer.

Meanwhile a comrade, having received the password and plan for seizure of the neighbouring police staton and all its arms, says with a note of deep regret:

"Mensch, den har ick dat jo nicht mehr neudig hat!" (Hell, this is no use to me any more!)

The entire Barmbeck struggle lasting three days was in its first phase directed towards the railway line, the spinal column of the area, which the workers could not smash due to insufficient weapons and principally through lack of explosives. The position was complicated by the fact that one of the most difficult police stations, Von-Essen Strasse, was situated in the rear of the insurgents and had not been captured by them: it drew off and pinned down considerable insurrectionary forces throughout the struggle. This station stayed intact by a complete accident. When C., an enormously big man distinguished by an unusually cool temper, as impervious and as well rolled as fresh asphalt, had with two comrades broken through the station's main entrance and rapped a stick on the table demanding immediate surrender, and the Blues and Greens* were already starting hesitantly to unfasten their stout belt-buckles, a second detachment from the unit came round from the back of the building, penetrated the yard and, puzzled by the utter silence reigning in the now occupied mouse-trap, opened fire at the station win-

---

* The Blues are the security police who wore blue uniforms while the Greens are probably Reichswehr soldiers. (R.C.)

dows. The Sipos and Reichswehr men came to their senses, saw three unarmed workers in front of them, threw two of them to the ground catching C. off guard, barred themselves in the cellar and showered the invaders with hand grenades. The workers' unit retreated. But at the very first intersection it was halted by Kb. who had already had his stubborn network of barricades put up to meet the troops.

One officer for the whole of the Hamburg Rising but how much he did for it! There was not a street in Barmbeck, not an alley, crack or chink not blocked up with a couple of plugs. Barricades seemed to sprout from the ground multiplying at an incredible rate. If there were no saws and spades, they were found. Residents were drawn into this excavation work: sweating, they dragged stones, broke up pavements and selflessly sawed up the sacred trees in the public gardens; they were ready to blow themselves to dust if that would save their cupboards, chests of drawers, beds and trunks from this frantic work of construction.

Only one old woman touched Kb.'s sleeve and beckoned him upstairs after her to take a wide sturdy board that was extremely handy for a barricade off her washstand — the pride of the whole household. The board was put into use and endured stoutly to the end — though this was an exception. The old romantic barricade has by and large had its day long ago. A girl in a Phrygian cap does not hold a tattered banner over it, Versaillaises in white gaiters no longer mow down the courageous *gamin* nor does the student from the Latin Quarter clutch his fatal wound in a lace handkerchief while a worker delivers his last bullet from the long old-fashioned barrel of the last pistol. Alas! The art of war has stuffed all this lovely romantic drivel back into the pages of school-books where it lives on tinged with the legends and powder-smoke of 1848. Today fighting is different. As a fortified wall between revolutionary rifles and government cannon the barricade long ago became a spectre. It no longer serves as a protection to anyone but solely as an impediment. It is a light wall assembled from trees, stones and upturned vehicles covering itself with a deep ditch, pit or trench that bars the way to armoured cars, those most dangerous foes of an uprising. It is in this trench that the meaning of the modern barricade's existence lies. But the old-time barricade, now backed up by the field-trench that has migrated to the city from the dead fields of large-scale warfare, continues to serve insurgents in all good faith even if it is in rather a different fashion from its heroic great-grandfathers of 1793 and 1848.

Piled up across the streets impeding a proper view of what is actually going on beyond its menacingly jagged wings it causes the enemy's attention to be focussed on it as his only visible target. The barricade courageously catches with its breast all the blind frenzied fire that troops rain down on their unseen enemy. Yes, here again is another new feature that has wholly changed the landscape of civil war and all its strategy and tactics. The workers have become invisible, elusive and almost invulnerable. For them the new method of warfare has devised a cap of darkness that no quick-firing weapon can reach. The workers fight rarely if at all in the streets, leaving these entirely to police and troops. Their new barricade, a huge stone one with millions of secret passageways and loop-holes is formed by the whole working-class area with all its basements, attics and living quarters: in this unassailable fortress every ground-floor window is an embrasure, every attic a battery and observation post. Every worker's bed is a litter which an insurgent can count on in the event of being wounded. It is only this that explains the utterly disproportionate government losses, whereas the workers in Barmbeck could count scarcely a dozen wounded and between two and five killed.

The troops were forced to advance along open streets. The workers joined battle from their homes. All attempts by the regular forces to take Barmbeck on Tuesday were thwarted by this same straggling, invisible, elusive formation of rifles which could coolly pick its targets from somewhere at a first floor window while down below the helplessly exposed crowd of police literally showered the empty barricades with fire.

Anticipating an armoured assault Kb. contrived to blow up

a concrete bridge, considered to be there for ever, with neither dynamite nor gunpowder. Workers felt out its vulnerable artery, the gas main, uncovered it and set it alight.

One of the vehicles blundered into a quiet deserted street. It stopped to put something right in the engine. A barricade sprouted in front of it. It turned round — the fallen crowns of sawn-down trees were already lying criss-crossed on the roadway.

Vehicle no. M-14 steals forward cautiously underneath the railway bridge. In it are the driver and five Sipos. From behind a pub or round a corner, it is not known from where, but close by, a shot and then another. The driver is killed and a policeman too. The vehicle is torn to shreds and the debris scattered about by Young Communists.

Veritable pitched battles continued all day Tuesday. The first heavy assaults can be placed at about eleven o' clock. The hardest fought of all were around the Von-Essen Strasse police station and along the whole line of barricades facing the railway embankment from both sides. The police quickly win the railway station. Their detachments run along the track trying to pick off the fighters from above. They are quietly drawn past the first two ambushes. Over the third span of the viaduct a deadly volley breaks out. They are firing not only from cover but from all the neighbouring attics. Riflemen have been sprinkled across the rooftops, keeping whole streets, the main intersections and squares under fire.

Below, an earthwork and a barricade. It has held now for several hours. A Sipo detachment moves against it even more savagely. The position becomes untenable. But from upstairs the cry: 'Die Barrikade frei' (Clear the barricades). The people don't realise what's going on. A marksman goes down to them, a worker of only about twenty-three, apparently wounded as his shoulder is bleeding — and his neck and waist. He gives the order to clear the barricade because the squad ensconced on the roof is afraid of hitting its own side. The worker disappears into a driveway and a few minutes later fire from the roof forces the police to retreat.

Another barricade that put up stubborn resistance for hours. A quartet of lone marksmen come downstairs from an attic.

From their observation turret they had already spotted an armoured car approaching from far away and decided that it would be more convenient to greet it downstairs. With a happy shot one of them manages to pierce the radiator, paralysing the vehicle. The riflemen return once more to their pigeon loft.

Meanwhile the battles at the railway station are flaring up even more. The workers not only succeed in dislodging several White columns one after the other from the embankment but attempt to go over to the offensive themselves. But the open space in front of the viaduct is under bombardment from armoured cars. It is impossible to pass. No matter, the workers confront the fire under cover of huge beams taken from a nearby timber yard. A whole forest of masts gets up and moves forward to form a perfect blockhouse from which the riflemen continue their steady methodical work.

At this point the first massed attack is unleashed below. Two armoured cars cover six lorries that toss a whole host of Greens on to the road. This unit succeeds in cutting off comrade K. from Kb. and his men moving up from the other side of the viaduct. Not only that. Kb., who has left his soldiers some two hundred metres behind, is captured. He is searched and locked up in the railway building. If only the police had known that in the figure of this puny man with the inoffensive eyes of a young teacher who might be rash enough to go out for a stroll among the barricades, they held in their hands the heart of Barmbeck in revolt. Sitting nice and quietly by a window Kb. conducted a general review of the enemy's forces. He watched exhorted mobs of police go past, urged on by the few courageous officers. Those hapless hirelings cheering themselves on with shots and cries, throwing themselves on their bellies every four paces, making desperate gestures towards a phlegmatic armoured car standing several metres behind its 'vanguard'. From that same window Kb. could also observe the cool self-possession of several workers, especially little D. whose handiwork he could tell from the terrified faces of the orderlies coming out of the fire eight times in a row with heavily swaying stretchers. Finally to the sound of convulsed shouts and firing the last platoon of Greens dis-

appeared down the empty streets of the insurgent quarter —
strange, absolutely empty streets, devoid of any sign of life
as if abandoned by occupants and defenders. The waiting lasts
for four endless agonising hours. At about five in the afternoon the
wave of troops and police rolls back noisily. Their losses are enormous.

Alas, the staff centre that was to have directed the Rising
in Barmbeck itself (led by three communist intellectuals, city coun-
cillors) is absent. For two days no one can find them anywhere. The
battles are directed by Kb., C. and of course T. who set himself up
with his wireless equipment right beneath the open sky in one of
the public parks.

At about six o'clock in the evening Barmbeck is still standing, deafened by the stillness — a respite. Kb. finds his way to a friendly pub where D., the little marksman, is by now lying on a settee
being fed with hot coffee. W., and that splendid marksman C. come
here for a breather too. And that impetuous K. is as warm and jolly
as if he has just been playing skittles in a pleasant after-dinner
break or has just completed one of his twenty-mile strolls dragging
a querulous exhausted wife along behind him; he chooses this spot
to give instructions to his workers' hundreds.

To sum up: all that was courageous in the Barmbeck pocket
came here to shake hands, wash the blood off and decide: what
now? What does this stillness mean, broken only occasionally by
the clatter of a sash out of which a white flag is flung into the
street — the appeal of someone wounded or dying?

Meanwhile silent Barmbeck, with twilight descending on
it like a foggy sheet on to the stretchers formed by the maimed
streets, is ever so quietly split into two halves. Fifteen hundred
troops separate North from South Barmbeck. The strong points, at
Wagnerstrasse, police station 46, Friedrichstrasse station and Pfen-
ningsbusch, silently stretch out their arms to each other in the darkness like a police cordon forcing back some innocuous street demonstration.

All of a sudden the ring snaps shut — a muscular elastic
ring in which the bulky forms of armoured cars once again drawn

up hard against the barricades are set like dull stones in a bracelet. A solid lump rolls up into Barmbeck's throat. True, our posts are still in place. But time is against them. The enemy is gaining with every drop of darkness that night is forcing between the quarter's fiercely locked teeth.

In the end the Whites are just as invisible, and therefore invulnerable, as the insurrectionaries. And there are more of them.

Along either side of one of the streets there creeps a double file of patrols. At some gateway the officer-in-charge grabs some innocently intellectual-looking man and jabs a revolver into his ribs. He does not see a second man who, with a rifle in his hands, has recoiled back into the dark and is as motionless as a stone. For the second time that day the *Landsknechte* (mercenaries) have caught hold of the mainspring of raging Barmbeck and then let it slip through their fingers. An hour and a half later Kb. was giving the order to his riflemen to melt away, disappear from Barmbeck, now encircled, half-strangled and half-inundated with torrents of unseen enemies.

Each cleared his own line of retreat independently; one took that mountain path across the rocky ridges of rooftops and over the gulleys in those man-made urban Alps. Not one put a foot wrong, not one was caught.

On the following morning all thirty-five had already met again in North Barmbeck and decided to dig in on the broad semicircle of the railway embankment. Again for a period of several long hours, battles, frenzied shooting, obstacles across the adjoining streets, barricades and many, many fallen enemy. Fifty fresh rifles enter service — alas, toy ones taken from a local club: and in the face of this Rising pressed up against the embankment on either flank, three defeated assaults, three hound-packs forced to depart with shattered skulls: that day cost the Reds four men. Four excellent comrades: and old Lewien paid for it in excruciatingly painful blood. The baby's rattles, the sportsmen's rifles from the club, were found in his garden. Old Mrs. Lewien, living in her little house with its antiquated chests-of-drawers, cat, white goat, portrait of Liebknecht the elder and the almost hundred-year-old tradition of

courageous atheism and the old party of the days of the Anti-Socialist Law, was first given back the old man's blood-stained overcoat
and then a completely bloodless body. His elder son, a philistine
and SPDer arrived to burrow through the boxes, sell off the chattels
and demand a signature on some papers from old Mrs. Lewien. But
she can recall one thing only: the old man standing alone on a lorry
in a crowd of Greens and that he was pale.

Here on the evening of the 24th the comrades learnt almost simultaneously of the fall of Schiffbek and the calm reigning
in the rest of Germany.

That Wednesday, the 24th, having received no news of the
start of the German revolution the leading group was compelled to
sound the retreat. Not because the workers had been smashed but
what was the point of pursuing the struggle in Hamburg alone, of
flaring up in isolation against a backcloth of general collapse?!

It was not quite so easy to order the retreat in a city drunk
with victory, where the defence is ready at any moment to go over
to the offensive and hundreds of barricades and tens of thousands
of workers are preparing for an all-out assault and the terrible closing act of civil war — the triumphant seizure of power. The first
courier who brought to the barricades the order to retreat was
knocked off his feet with a furious punch. He was an honest old
worker who, together with his family had maintained the dangerous courier service throughout the Rising. When he thought of that
terrible punch so unjustly received from his comrades Comrade P. almost did himself in, becoming as bloodshot as that battered cheek
of his. In just the same way all working-class Hamburg clutched its
jaw and turned blind with the pain when it received the order to liq-
uidate the Rising. You had to enjoy the confidence of the masses
such as T. did having grown up with his organisations and being so
inextricably linked to their proletarian core that he could make the
abrupt swing of helm to demobilisation with impunity.

All right, they retreated. Disappointed and grumbling,
parting for the last time yet having repulsed the enemy from their
barricades for many hours. Taking advantage of the confusion the
riflemen abandoned the earthworks, barricades and sentry posts

without a sound. They went off with their weapons taking with them the dead and wounded, covering up all traces left behind them, and gradually scattered out into the now silent suburbs. This planned retreat was carried out under the cover of marksmen dispersed on the roofs. None of them left his aerial barricade until five floors below the last fighter had left his trench and the last casualty, supported under the arms by his comrades, had hidden himself behind the gateway of a safe house. They held on all day, all the while holding down the Whites, running across from one zone to another, along slippery cornices hanging over ravines, past black staircases gaping like trenches, past wells and dormer windows through which the police ever more insistently surged upwards as they finally scented emptiness and defeat behind the unmanned hushed barricades. The struggle had turned into a chase. The whole population concealed and saved the heroic rearguard of the Hamburg October, those wounded, blackened hounded loners still firing somewhere over the city and then suddenly digging themselves into some unknown working-class family; dressed in rags, with bloodied hands, parched black mouths and a pack of huntsmen careering, roaring and swearing past the scarcely slammed door.

One of the last to retreat was the old party comrade W. who, tottering with fatigue and drunk with a desire to lie down and sleep, could no longer cling to a slippery tile or the corner of a sharp chimney. At last when down below an exit to freedom had opened up before him in the shadow of some murky gateway, he stopped again and unslung his rifle to let off his last cartridges with a malicious glee. The whole corner on which he was leaning had been lacerated with bullets. By sheer chance not one of them had grazed his head, now against the stonework a shadow wreathed with scratches and holes. They only just managed to get him away. Around his neck over an unbuttoned shirt and a shaggy sweaty chest a dazzlingly smart tie was fastened.

"What's this *Schlips* (tie) on for, old chap?"

"Ich wollte festlich sterben." (I wanted to die properly.)

Schiffbek

Lying a little way out of Hamburg where a dreary line of telegraph poles marches off in the direction of flat, denuded sandy Prussia is a small working-class town by the name of Schiffbek. It ranges out between the Bille brook, murky and smooth as tinplate, and hills on which grow sparse trees that have run bare-headed and tousled into the wind and also assorted little two-storey houses of a workers' settlement.

In the centre the evangelical church stands empty like a rusty umbrella stuck into the ground to dry out after the rain and forgotten there for ever. Not believing in God the cosmopolitan population of this working-class town does not visit it. Today, after the battles, it stands there with a black eye, without window-panes or doors — a priest who has strayed and ended up in someone else's fight.

A large chemical factory stands on a little island on the far side of the Bille: cold, venomous and full of crystals that are deposited into the icy black water, naphthaline and green poisons that seem to cover the river-bed with a film of fresh vitriolic moss. Some thousand workers are employed there.

Inside the kilns that never cool off fire that is as dense as the molten planets is poured out. It is observed through tiny windows. Sometimes the white heat is coated with a light coaly haze but more often it is as white and still as blindness. Naked to the waist, workers charge away from the blazing kilns out into the frost, snow or rain to escape an atmosphere in which the one-time gigantic mare's-tails and warm swamps that are now stacked in the corners as heaps of coal might have grown and revelled.

Along either side of a narrow stone corridor lies a steam-mill and a huge iron-rolling works. On Christmas Eve its chimney, higher than all the others, is like a sullen smoker left suddenly without tobacco.

'Tin Shacks' are spread out along the fringe of the now frozen white waste patches. This works has one long legless body pressing its belly against the ground and seven equally tall chimneys set in a row like minarets from which every morning a shrill muezzin of labour sounds.

Work at this factory is extremely damaging to the lungs. The toughest cannot stand more than four years of it. You have to be like S., a hero of the Hamburg Rising, to emerge unharmed after working several years in the inferno. But then S. is a giant whose build all Schiffbek is proud of.

Ask any little urchin and he will tell you that S. can lift on his shoulder six men clinging to an iron crowbar, that his hands are much bigger and can hold much more than the purses that the good housewives of Schiffbek take to market and that in the morning when he swings his extraordinary legs out of bed the whole tenement creaks and shakes so much that neighbours without watches know it is time to wake their husbands for work. So then as we have said, since S. is such a colossus, a bold spirit, a Bolshevik and generally devilish the 'Tin Shacks' have not done him too much harm. But little C. came out of them with a leg seared to the bone; K. with red spittle wrapped up in his dirty handkerchief.

Further up the Bille stand the smoky towers of Jute, one of Hamburg's largest manufacturing plants. It is predominantly women who work here; poorly remunerated and poorly organised, for whom the party has year after year conducted a bitter struggle against the Menshevik trade unions, the women's remarkably clamorous, inflammable but easily intimidated inertness, the employer and the priest.

The Jute women doggedly resisted any stable organisation. Where possible they would moan about their wages and after the first few days of a strike would go whining to make peace with the manager, first smashing the office windows and then informing on the instigators. However, the factory, in the course of its normal capitalist business, is itself combing out of this tangled, unexacting, conveniently exploitable, female mass the first strands of a strong proletarian solidarity. Amenable as the women might have been their wages still slipped down and down. First one department and then another was subjected to the frantic inflationary race of prices and wages. Yet within the bounds of their own homes, their own housekeeping and their own factory the women remain as united as they are indifferent to political movements that go beyond those bounds. They may not take any notice of a General Strike but they will never let their workmates down in the next section. Thus, for over a year now, the basically peaceable Jute has, thank goodness, worked no more than three days out of six: the rest of the time the factory is out in the street supporting the section on strike at the particular time.

"O, ha!" (that is a pet expression of every true Hamburger).

"O, ha!" say the workers who have been conducting propaganda at the Jute factory for months and years, "hunger is making good communists of them".

Here is one of the astonishing women to have come out of the Jute. Let's call her Elfriede and say that she is the daughter of a Schiffbek night-watchman. Father was well-known about the town as an orthodox Menshevik and the owner of a superb carbine with which he maintained order and tranquillity in the derelict areas and buildings in his care called *Hundebuden* (dog-kennels) by the workers. And so it was.

But if the watchman faithfully upheld the law of private property with his carbine then Elfriede in every way overturned and trampled down those sacred bastions with her amazing beauty.

Elfriede was not only a perfect communist, an excellent workmate and a heroic girl who fought at the barricades, raising

Schiffbek's entire female population to its feet to set up field kitchens and herself taking out under fire hot coffee and fresh cartridges fastened around her slim waist to the marksmen in the trenches; with her own hands she put her old man under lock and key adding his old-fashioned rifle to the party's scanty war material and was finally caught by the police in the heat of her criminal activity, namely while cleaning potatoes for the insurgents with her sleeves rolled up amid piles of fresh peelings; not only was she a courageous active woman for ever dedicated to the party but also perhaps one of the first examples of a new brave type so unsuccessfully faked in the pages of the neo-proletarian novel and the homilies of armchair revolutionaries.

There came with her into the poverty-stricken district of Schiffbek the spirit of destruction and liberty. Elfriede refused to become anyone's wife. Her name evoked the timid respect and furious hatred of legal wives whose husbands she would take away for a day, a year or for life, of fathers and lovers.

She would conquer whomever she chose, make love for as long as there were no lies in that loving and then haughtily return her captive to freedom. But she asked no one for a name, a shield or aid for herself or her child. Never, neither in weakness nor in sickness, did she seek support in the law that all her life she had despised.

From the bench she went to jail.

But first a scene, an astonishing scene that actually took place in a corridor of the Hamburg City Hall from whose balcony Doctor Laufenberg was carefully thrown in 1918 and where arrested communists were brought on 23 October.

On that dreadful day there stood in the forecourt of Schiffbek police station in rows of three, four or five, lorries loaded with captured workers lying on their backs, heaped on top of each other.

The rebels! They had fought in open battle according to all the rules of honest warfare, pitting life against life with an adversary a hundred times stronger, yet still sparing prisoners and letting the wounded go. After the defeat they were of course treated like hunted ruffians, renegades standing outside the law. The police pounded their feet on those rows of bloody, gasping bodies heaped upon each other. Dying men crushed by their comrades on top lay underneath with faces squashed against the coal-smeared boards while above the *Wachtmeister* (sergeants) of the Reichswehr tugged hair out and with their rifle-butts cracked the napes of the immobilised men who then lost consciousness.

Three men were overwhelmed there. S., that oak among men, a superman in his astounding physical strength, spewed blood and lost his senses. K. was dying and agile little L. beneath his pacifier's boot was ready to leap out of his crushed existence just as an eye slips from its socket full of fire and tears. About all this later: I don't wish to start on Schiffbek with the phase of police atrocities. They are merely a bloody and dirty epilogue to three days of the Rising that cannot be stamped out by a soldier's boot from the history of a new working-class humanity. For indeed how unattainable is the shining peak on which stands the struggle of Hamburg labour above the bloody filth of police station floors, the vile courtroom offices where the proceedings were written out and torn up, torn up and re-written, the reeking stifling lavatories of that now illustrious City Hall where the arrested were forced to wash and even take a shower so that members of the city government, and Messrs. socialist deputies who had come to be convinced of the police's kind and humane treatment of its prisoners-of-war, did not become queasy at the sight of the blood smeared everywhere or the smell of the clothes of an adolescent member of the Hamburg Young Communists, beaten until he had lost control of his physiological functions.

So it was that in that long white corridor where the drunken soldiery drove the living piece of revolution that had fallen back through the lines into its hands, men cowered by the walls under the lash and it smelt of rubber and blood, in that corridor Elfriede who had so zealously and laboriously upheld her lonely dignified life free from the prop of any official morality, yet as pure and as straight as an arrow, in that corridor she was swamped with the foulest, filthiest abuse and mockery.

Every quarter of an hour a new group of Reichswehr burst

into the hall, picked up off the floor those who had already collapsed, beat up again those who had already been beaten up, revived those who had fainted so as to knock them down again and then each of those gangs started once again on her standing as if naked among wild beasts.

"Communist slut," they shouted.

"Whore," they shouted.

"You're not a German woman but an animal," they shouted.

And in that ghastly interminable torture-chamber that lasted a day, a night and another day, this girl recalled: yes, there had been a great German woman, as great as a marble statue, and nothing since her ghastly death had been quite so fine and wise in the German revolution.

And what's more she had left behind a small book of letters. A white cover with red lettering. Letters from prison.

Rosa Luxemburg.

Elfriede stood in that satanic corridor and cried out about Rosa Luxemburg until she was heard. When a girl arms herself with Rosa's name she is as powerful and as dangerous as an armed man — she is a warrior and no one will dare touch her.

It is impossible to pick up what she said and how or what her words were.

But some N.C.O. made an apology.

One of the gangs went off with tails between their legs saying that 'they hadn't known'. Perhaps this interval was used to get one of the injured men away from the soldiers and drag him out of the scrum by the arm.

That is the tale of Elfriede from Schiffbek.

Portraits

1. A Pair

A couple. In Schiffbek they tell how there lived this pair, husband and wife, both fine old communists. Several years ago they separated, led independent lives with new families and did not meet each other. A superb marksman, he was fighting in October in one of the trenches that intersected the narrow bare little streets. It so happened that his former wife was standing there fighting next to him. As before — in the days of the Spartacus Rising and the Kapp putsch. The worker was caught and his wife gave herself up the next day. And so that family of fighters re-united quite naturally at the first shot, under fire. They will stand trial together.

2. A Private House and the Rising

She was a short-sighted, normal, chaste Catholic nurse with poor eyesight. Today after the war he is a communist. A remarkable resourceful, earnest quick worker. He plugged into the party like those tiny household batteries that can give light, turn a roller to sharpen knives or can, in eights, drive a model railway and yet which remain but miniatures or an enormous miracle of energy, the motor of a whole era of machines but on a minuscule scale. When necessary the little battery can emit real burning sparks bigger than itself.

This practical-minded highly-skilled worker was struck down with a rather special and rare illness that takes one in ten thousand and is thus incurable: he was struck with a great and tormenting love for the devout, bony gawky nurse.

As is normal in such cases it set in quite mutually and in one minute they were transfixed.

They got married, vaulting over his politics and her catechism and even forgot about them for a while. Then, comrade L., who never flagged and never moved away from the party, started to save money to build his own little house on the outskirts of the outskirts, beyond the oasis of little white houses with red roofs that members of the local authority, five old Mensheviks, had donated themselves out of official funds. All in one spot, just like one big family.

The wind gusts around them and the population passing by spits. Anyway these people are living well and contentedly.

L. worked; he worked overtime and nights and on his days off he would rush down to the site to erect his house with great patience and toil: brick by brick, chip by chip, tile by tile.

The first baby came along and the second one too. The party faded into a mist and became a theoretical outlook on life, an idea locked away in an unoccupied corner.

Sometimes, in moments of domestic repose L. could hear its monotonous tread and feel it standing and listening at the door of his conscience.

The short-sighted industrious wife finally could start living in her own home, to sew by her own brightly scrubbed fireplace, sleep in her own bed, rear children, wash down the stove's Dutch tilework, wash the little piglets and wash the gleaming floors. On Sundays L. would now read aloud some romance of court life about the objectionably pampered child of a count — with a wedding at the end.

On the morning of 23 October L. had just stuck the pig for Christmas. The blood had already been drained off into a barrel for the black pudding. At that moment the shooting started. In spite of the house he had put up with his own hands and pasted together with the sweat of his brow, in spite of that extraordinary love for his wife, the communist took his rifle and went. And then what happened?

He was captured, beaten up and released. A trial in a few days' time. So what then? Stay at home or flee?

That same powerful revolutionary instinct that had previously driven L. to the barricades now drove this well-set up, bourgeoisified, domesticated German worker out into the streets amidst the cross-currents of bullets whizzing past the corners of the workers' tenements and the wretched covers; to confront the two thousand regular troops who stormed this hornet's nest to take it empty. Ruthless class instinct now commanded: do not leave the party any more, do not dare desert, you must go underground and go on with the work.

But on the day following his flight the house and the belongings, even Lumpi the guard dog, will be confiscated by the government. The wife, two children and the newly-born third will find themselves turned out into the street. Besides, for some reason his wife is going blind and has started to pray often and at length.

Nevertheless one night they arrived at C.'s — she without hat or glasses — and recounted their whole life to the comrade, including that wonderful first look that had at one time decided their fate.

The next day L. made off.

3. The Eighteenth Century, the Joy of Living and the Rising

Actually this portrait does not concern the history of the Rising itself. But there is invariably in every gallery as a matter of course 'Das Bildnis eines Unbekannten' (the portrait of an unknown man) and such an anonymous sketch can often tell more about the inimitable peculiarities of its period than all the signed canvasses.

We have to draw a house, a sunken ship slowly settling down somewhere on the seabed, in a dark side-street where from time to time it is flooded with light from the white eyes of a motor car drifting past. The lamp over the gate radiates a light resembling the glow of a rotting tree.

A stinking gateway and windows close to the ground for ever eavesdropping on each other.

The bedroom, as cold as the North Pole with its numbed window-panes, cupboard and gaping wash-basin, warms itself on a hot-water bottle stuffed under an icy feather-bed. In the dining-room — which is also the sitting-room and workshop — is the dense but rapidly escaping warmth of an iron stove; on the lamp a gawdy silk shade looking like some cheap tart's petticoat; in the kitchen a reeking sink, gas and the heavy smell of dampness. The whole setting testifies to the indubitable prosperity of an aristocratic worker: it belongs to comrade K., an artist in wood. He is employed in one of the biggest furniture factories that make and imitate antique pieces. His speciality is the eighteenth century which, without ever having read anything about art, he feels to the tips of his fingers. With his eyes shut the master can impeccably saw out the cherry-coloured veneer inlaid with metal and tortoise-shell and the furniture whose effete intricate gently-curving contours emerge from a deal board, a heavy moist piece of wood that has fallen into these amazingly creative hands, as effortlessly as if they had come from the workshop of the celebrated Boulle. In each of the old-fashioned writing desks at which, presumably, our grandmothers wrote their love letters, and in each of the card-tables on which the Werthers broke their chalk scribbling out the names of their beloveds after having placed a candle beside the weighty pistols, K., the craftsman, fits, for the sake of style, secret drawers, little recesses and hidden springs that, if accidentally pressed, deliver into the hands of the admirable bourgeois a couple of yellowing papers, a bunch of dried forget-me-nots and that most rare aroma of someone else's secret. All these items have been gleaned by that same craftsman K. with enormous taste and sense of proportion.

Communism has for him been tucked away like a casket full of ideas, words and generalities wholly inapplicable to practical life that form the most priceless and intimate thing in life — political style.

Need it be said that in the Rising K. took no active part unless of course you count the broad hospitality he extended to comrades following the battles.

K. is an Epicurean. A true Renaissance man in his effervescent irrepressible love of life, its pleasures and its palpably warm human beauty, his sense of which is as infallible as his cabinet-maker's skill. K. believes that the very process of life with all its physiological and profoundly mundane functions will some day become the basis for the greatest and truest beauty. This social aesthetic gives him an affinity with the best things that Edgar Allan Poe wrote about — the as yet non-existent gardens and palaces to be inhabited by wise men. K. populates them with workers.

'If the kingdom of the future were suddenly to arrive' (again a purely German concept: only a utopian who does not believe in his day-dream could express himself that way) he would fashion wonderful shelves, beds, tables and chairs for the workers' palaces. This is his ideal communist 'casket'.

But now the practice. Why did he not join the fight in October? Why does he smile when you talk about strikes and distributing leaflets? Given all this deliberate passivity and indisputable desertion from the field of civil war where does that provocative arrogance and manner of a victor over the bourgeoisie come from? Why in the end did this man, who was created for great spiritual and physical pleasures and who thought communism the only road by which he and his class could attain such pleasures, not lift a single finger or once risk his neck during the Rising?

It turns out that he is thieving and plundering his bourgeois. He is stealing almost openly, stacking away sums large by the standards of cottage industry, putting unimaginable profits into his pocket while looking provocatively into his boss's eye and keeping a watch on the cowardly accomplices who assist him. Then after a week of the most arduous labour, working a ten-hour day with continuous strain, come several bottles of excellent beer, his little wife Eisa in her black silk underwear and, from out of the stinking corner where the Roederer's cork hits the low ceiling like a tall man who has wandered in and banged himself against the bank of this pit, through the haze of a strong cigar, through the fog of perspiring, sultry dampness, through the golden illusions bursting in tiny bubbles on the surface of the earthenware mug in which centenarian grape fizzes, comrade K., with the smirk of a conqueror, contemplates the bourgeoisie he has deceived, deceived so cunningly and boldly.

Those are his finest hours.

The old songs of Hamburg are older and more rollicking than ours. There is one about a craftsman's daughter who loved three boisterous apprentices thrown out by her father, another about sea-horses and women, about brawls and dockside pubs. He sings them marvellously.

How do you tell K. that for the crumbs the boss permits his irreplaceable craftsman to snatch off his plentiful table, the drop of stolen wine and those few hours' blessed oblivion, he is as much giving his enemy the marrow of his bone, his life and the mysterious trembling fibres of the brain that we call talent as any labourer gives his sweat, muscle and bones?

Schiffbek

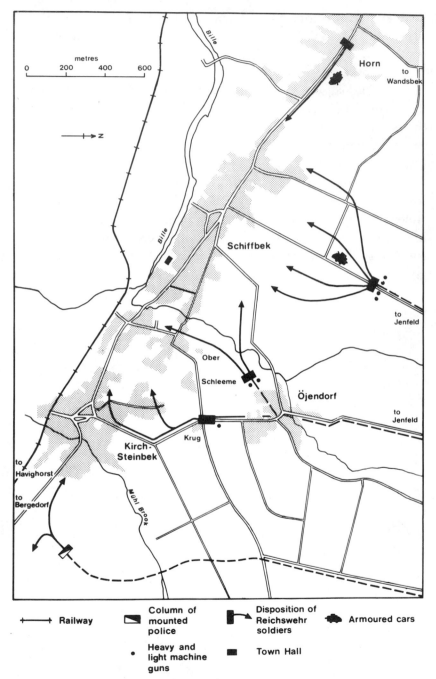

metres
0   200   400   600

Bille

Horn

to
Wandsbek

Schiffbek

to
Jenfeld

Ober
Schleeme

Öjendorf

to
Jenfeld

Kirch-
Steinbek

Krug

to
Havighorst

to
Bergedorf

Mühl Brook

┼──► Railway	Column of mounted police	Disposition of Reichswehr soldiers	Armoured cars
•	Heavy and light machine guns	Town Hall	

About Schiffbek Again

Schiffbek's police station, council offices, post office and in general all the institutions and public buildings that personify state power in this small working-class town with its cosmopolitan population were seized by the communists at dawn on 23 October with the aid of one carbine and one hunting knife with a serrated blade and a horn handle.

As in the rest of Hamburg, Schiffbek police station, packed as it was with armed Sipos, was taken by surprise with bare hands, quickly and without a sound. At the head of the whole Rising and of the military organisation that worked out and implemented its plan was S. A giant and a brave man, one of those truly revolutionary workers of whom modern Germany can be proud. Perhaps it was that very physical strength and an awareness that with one movement of his metallic muscles he could crush any adversary that had developed in him that sense of caution so valuable to a leader and an ability to calculate the precise effect of every discharge of force. He could come down like a steam-hammer on an anvil carefully splitting a nutshell without damaging the kernel — and a minute later beat out an iron bar.

His armed squad, formed of picked members of the local organisation, stood and fought just as S. himself would fight: when surrounded on all sides by an invading mob and pinned against a wall he would knock those small fry off their feet one by one without checking the incredible reach and power of his hammer-fists.

Having occupied the police station the Schiffbek insurgents did not remain there but, seizing sixteen rifles and as many revolvers, left the building which could have become the same trap for them as it had been for the police they had just seized and disarmed.

One good marksman, by concealing himself behind the shrubs, garden sheds and corners of the workers' barracks scattered along the length of the hills on the left-hand side of the central highway linking Schiffbek with Hamburg, could and did keep the road, bridge and railway embankment under fire and hold at a respectable distance an enemy ten, a hundred, and finally, during the last assaults of the morning of the 26th, a thousand times stronger.

A marksman, or, as they are called here, *Scharfeschütze*, would, by remaining secure behind his cover and firing at long intervals, every five, ten or fifteen minutes, attempt to pick off at least one, and often two men with a single bullet. To these isolated and always lethal shots the police replied by sweeping whole blocks with drum-fire from their machine-guns — they mowed down a multitude of women and children that had accidentally fallen within the sights of their impotent rage. Nevertheless, after a brief lull, a cold, calculated sharp-eyed shot again rang out, catching the driver of an armoured car who had just peeped out from under the steel hatch, removed a fur mitten and lit up a cigarette with relief, a Green who had leapt out from round a corner and a Reichswehr soldier squatting behind a letter box who had just stopped in the middle of the street a tram conductor's wife, whose face and loaf tucked under her kerchief had seemed to him suspicious.

Reichswehr soldiers are recruited from among clumsy country lads. They are the younger sons of rich peasants, a generation that matured after the war and revolution. In the countryside they are a burden on their fathers; greedy, lazy, pampered farmhands who will not put sufficient horsepower into the land as they cannot count upon an inheritance in the future. Such lads, political quadrupeds, readily become Landsknechte and look upon civil war as a pogrom in the course of which they stand to gain much with little risk. But instead of unarmed women and children terrorised in bread queues and that cowardly city rabble of whom back at home the priest with his plump chin resting on his white collar would tell with such passion, the well-fed little peasants stumbled against workers' hundreds and the cold-blooded, flawless fire of old soldiers who had come out of the world war with every badge of distinction for accurate marksmanship and sapper work under enemy machine-gun fire.

The roles have been reversed. In Germany the revolution draws upon cadres of old soldiers who defend their barricades according to all the rules of military science while the government has numerous but totally inexperienced and untempered units, cowardly in battle though brutal when facing a captive with his hands tied behind his back. It was not by chance that one of the officers found it necessary to drive his detachment of raw recruits forward into the attack revolver in hand just to smoke out a lone rifleman ensconced in the attic of his house who was faultlessly picking off one soldier after another; as he urged his cannon fodder on this lieutenant swore aloud before the whole town:

"You scum of the earth, you cowards . . . With twenty of them (a motion towards the dormer window) I could sort out thousands like you!"

But even without the officer's assistance the Schiffbek workers, under the command of their S. and his Chief of Operations and Chief of Staff, the incomparable Fritz, resisted the onslaught of the regular troops. Adapting themselves to the conditions of the locality they would constantly switch their tactics. Where hills dominated the town or where the houses stood like oases amid open wastes they split their forces into small combat formations, each of which would defend itself at its own risk and peril, advance, take cover and change from one ambush to another. But where empty white fields flowed between narrow banks of the town's streets they relied upon the old and proven technique of street barricades, blocking the water-courses of the streets with firm dams and excavating earthworks so preventing armoured cars from breaking through to the central blocks.

At half past eleven the police, now in possession of the

empty police station, opened their first offensives against Schiff-bek. A detachment of fifty men advanced confidently along the main street; knocking down a few chance passers-by they moved up to a white building with a long stairway jutting out. Beautiful dark-eyed Minna went past the soldiers showing her gleaming teeth and making a count of the invaders. They did not even notice the red badge on her ample bosom. Her headscarf tied at the back disap-peared calmly down a side-street. A boy, a pupil at the town school, who had been running along beside her, turned round, hiccupped and sat down on the pavement. A bullet had struck him between the eyebrows.

In the insurgents' camp there was still the deepest silence until, at a distance of only twenty paces, several shots knocked the sergeant-major and half the soldiers out of the invading detach-ment.

An hour later, police now numbering some two hundred, moved in not just along one line but from several angles simultane-ously. The workers drove them back from their barricades and earthworks; from all the covers scattered along the hills they plas-tered the invaders with volley-fire. Fritz, the marksman, shot at the police from round the corner of his own tenement, surrounded by women holding the supplies of cartridges in torn aprons. A classic figure: a large-peaked cloth cap tied down with a scarf under the chin, a jacket in tatters and beneath it a heavy grey docker's jersey. His hair, which to this day that beautiful Minna cannot recall with-out laughter, is like a bandit's: after five minutes' wait one, just one shot. With it Fritz had picked off four of them.

It should be said that Schiffbek is rich in, and renowned for, its Fritzes. A second one directed the defence of the barricades and earthworks. Beside S. he is almost short. But while S. had grown ha-phazardly, branching out on all sides with a good-natured, powerful voluble crown right up in the sky, Fritz is a squat shrub firmly grip-ping the earth somewhere between the stones under a strong sea breeze. Heels together, a drum-like chest with his hands in pockets and one shoulder a little bit forward, the shoulder of a trained boxer and athlete at that. A whistle, insolent jibes and the ability to make a woman or a policeman blush equally — by looking them up and down. In addition an audacity that had won him the untranslatable nickname of *Didlein* — a nickname both contemptuous and flattering that means chap, rascal, smart alec, bold spirit, liar, gunman, rogue and pastry-cook — in fact a generally good fellow. In peaceful times this Fritz had rather shocked the sedate party functionaries with his sharp dockside smell and provocative unruly spirit but in the days of battle he worked miracle after miracle. He would rush from window to window, urge on, hold back, switch forces, swear and give commands as the ganglion between S.'s calm strength and all the roving knots of insurrectionaries.

At half past one the government crept towards Schiffbek with five hundred men plus a squadron of armoured cars. The fray lasted until six o'clock that evening. Two first-rate marksmen may well be able to stand fast for a long while but in the end courage and tenacity have their limits. In order to win time the combatants very quietly left the earthworks, dived through the nearest gateway and an hour and a half later the steel noses of their rifles were poking over the edge of another barricade, successively joining battle in the most hard-pressed areas.

Meanwhile the bewildered enemy was still flooding the now silent ambush with fire. From time to time the heat subsided; the blind barrage would break off and a scout crawl along the pavement on all fours. But then, from somewhere in a nearby attic a solitary shot quacks out and the bombardment is resumed with renewed force against the empty pit full of cartridge-cases, debris and charred soil. In the end the lieutenant seizing his revolver with a heroic flourish led forth his musketeers into the assault. Shooting blindly into the air and uttering war cries they tumbled into the empty ditch.

Dusk was falling. Sunset like a sentry sloped its long pointed bayonet-like shadows across all the streets. A poster had already appeared on Schiffbek's hoardings proclaiming a general strike and greeting the Soviet government. The thirty-five communists, beset by thousands of soldiers, were sure that all Germany was rising behind them. However, even without appeals the whole population supported the communists. Eight thousand people turned out on to the streets and if they did not take part in the struggle it was simply due to the total lack of weapons.

But the sacred intelligentsia! It is worth noting that in little Schiffbek, just as it used to be in Russia and everywhere else where the social revolution ultimately takes up arms, the intellectuals fire alongside the police and soldiers. Not a professor — for what professors are there in Schiffbek! — nor a teacher, — the teachers are well-meaning though timid — nor even a midwife — in Schiffbek women bear their own children without a hint of medical aid — but only an aged school janitor to make a stand for the fruits of European enlightenment. Left alone in his deserted premises, the wretched sixty-year-old, his head sated with schoolroom wisdom, a worker who had learnt to despise corns, the stench of poverty and muscular young ignorance as deeply as he himself was despised by the implacable blackboards, teachers' uniforms and plaster sages on the bookcase in the headmaster's study, this old janitor grabbed his pistol and decided to fire upon his own class, the pupils who were studying street disorder instead of penmanship and the Holy Writ.

A knock outside the door. The janitor hid. They knocked once more and then the gates left their hinges beneath S.'s angry shoulder. Then, raising one arm as on the Schiller memorial, looking comical and menacing with his hair dishevelled, the old man fired at the worker's broad chest and missed. Here the majestic posture ended. The janitor made for the stairs with S. after him. S. climbed up despite the drawn pistol and bellowed across the entire establishment:

"Crazy old *Karnikel* (bunny). You just empty the chamberpots to support their learning!"

"What use are you to anyone?!" and he removed the revolver from Uncle Paulus.

The old man wept most bitterly, for the years in which he had rubbed the white algebra and time-charts off the blackboards had made a true intellectual of him: the desperate frantic martyrdom and then the impotent tears proved it.

S. clipped him one round the head and let him off. This was

the situation: S., laughing and swearing dreadfully, holding the old man and his unfortunate weapon in one hand while he wiped the soot off his face that had been scorched by the shot. Amid tears Paulchen was forced to tear his old and desecrated party card to shreds.

All around: urchins, shooting, death and laughter.

By evening the battles had abated. The workers were forced to retreat — to this day S. will talk about this with utter shame and child-like vexation — to retreat five hundred paces from their old positions. That was on the Hamburg flank. But in the rear troops had managed to penetrate as far as the main square where wealthy residents showered them with sausages, margarine and congratulations. The encirclement closed in threatening to become a stranglehold. A squad of insurgents coming to the rescue from shattered Barmbeck could not break through the police blockade. By now vehicles of the military command were racing through the streets of Hamburg: General Staff officers rushed to inspect the network of barricades and found their positioning to be superb.

At daybreak workers were again lying in the trenches, attics and behind every possible cover. But the enemy whose three assaults had been smashed the day before, did not show himself. Hooters started wailing continuously and pointlessly from a few factories. Patrols paced up and down at the end of every side-street emptying into the fields relieving each other regularly. They were standing guard over the barricades from afar as if over a captive prisoner. Then, a menacing stillness. At first they were heartened by it. Then perturbed. And then they sensed enormous danger creeping up on Schiffbek from those silent wastes and made ready to meet it.

Thirty-five against five thousand.

At about one o'clock a unit of four armoured cars and six lorries appeared from the direction of Horn dropping a large contingent of Sipos on the road. From Uhlenfeld in the north twenty-six lorry-loads of Greens. From the direction of Eimsbüttel, cavalry. An aeroplane came down very low and flew over Schiffbek raking its already bullet-riddled walls with a grey curtain of bullets.

Although beaten by the Allies the German Army goes gallantly to war against its own proletarians. But the example is evidently infectious for it is now the workers who sting the government forces. Cavalry, infantry, armoured cars, aircraft and, on the polluted little river Bille, a whole navy made up of five launches of river police while a handful of workers, scoffing at this technology and the bloated, rotten shell of that hired army living off the employers' fat tips, continued to hold out until four o'clock in the afternoon. In the end, having thrown the troops back along sprawling unprotected fronts, beleaguered Schiffbek, driving before it crumpled up, broken columns of blue, green and other valiantly coloured soldiers, breaks through the ring of ambushes and emerges weapons in hand to freedom through that bloody breach. It's funny to relate: three riflemen form the rearguard of this miniature workers' army. They keep the 'Naval Forces of the Republic' at a respectable distance while S. and his men make their way into the country along the narrow gap between the river and the main highway.

Then the victors' celebration. The pandemonium of denunciations, searches, brutalities, arrests and church services. All this goes on for nearly two months. Dozens of workers are set outside the law. Many are arrested and await trial. Their families continue to tuck themselves away in the dank workers' barracks: one by one the insurgents' wives are thrown out of the factories on to the streets. Now and then a fast-talking trade-union leader appears at their homes: swollen and yellow with iodine and his head swathed in white. He had been seized near the 'Tin Shacks' during the Rising and beaten to mincemeat by the police in error. Now he replaces knocked-out teeth, conducts espionage and operates as a go-between.

Hunger, snows, dirty icy beds, the rent, the caretaker shouting and winter, beating its white birch rods on the road between your own little den that smells of gas, the lavatory and slushy filth, and the labour exchange. The exchange is a grey building standing to attention and saluting an open field. The back of this constable who has nodded off on duty is plastered with our proclamations.

From time to time the women who have been subjected to

every kind of pressure and every kind of privation are confronted by a police search-party or a pencil-and-paper gendarme for questioning. And then all that helpless poverty bristles its spines and puts up the stiffest and most courageous resistance to both the civil and the military power as they rattle their ringing broadswords outside on the staircase slippery with frozen slops.

The wife of a Schiffbek insurgent presses her arms to her sides, her face red with anger, the stove or the wash-tub and with yelling at screaming children and the shaggy dog that is furiously barking under the sagging settee, raises her voice to a shrill, rasping pitch and pushes away the papers laid before her as if brushing aside the obstinate perspiring hair from her brow; she vehemently denies and dodges and will not put her name to anything anywhere. Her abuse flies irresistibly down on to the heads of the departing officialdom as if tipped out of a rubbish bin. These women, for whom there is nothing to eat and who tomorrow will be thrown out of their lairs, push the police around, contemptuously pillorying them with their caustic jeers.

On Christmas Eve they get together to sew dozens of dolls for the children of communists who have fled. C. fashions a dolls' house out of old boxes pasting them over with newspaper and grubby kings and queens from long ago cast-off suits.

Hungry neighbours come round with presents — a bar of soap, a doll or a pair of warm stockings.

Finally, at night, a detachment of workers from Hamburg with a wheel-barrow of flour and margarine from American comrades. Fifty kilos of fat and twenty-five pounds of sugar for seventy families each numbering three to five mouths.

Hunger reaches its apogee several days before Christmas. Following an offer from a Dutch branch of Workers' International Relief Schiffbek is to send fifty of its children to Holland to be boarded out with foreign comrades.

A knock at the door — some workers arrive with embarrassed faces; they look at nothing but the washing hanging out over the cold stove or the syphilitically green wall and ask about the weather, their health and this and that.

From the vacant-eyed mother it is ascertained: whom they should take, a boy or a girl and how old? A quarter of an hour to get ready. No luggage. A few minutes' bitter howling on mother's shaking knees. But the stockings are by now firmly laced up, all buttons properly fastened and mother combs her daughter's tousled crop with brusque, peremptory movements that are at the same time dilatory and secretly drawn out. A quarter of an hour later the child is for ever ripped from its roots in routed Schiffbek.

Two mothers did not wish to give up their children.

One, burdened with four boys, two girls (her husband had been arrested and her factory had turned her out) and a window with newspaper instead of glass, keeps the six mouths above the water-line by means of unimaginable economies. The other is at the summit of filth, light-heartedness, jollity and physical ruin. Children of every complexion from many ardently, if briefly, loved fathers. The little girls come into the world, unasked for, yet in splendour, just as a wonderful golden-yellow sunflower appears on a dump from a seed accidentally fallen on a litter-strewn patch of ground. The little boys are hale and bright and once left to themselves they will be like the firm green spikes of a maple grasping the mould and flesh of an old factory wall with its squat trunk. Amid tears, curses and swearing at her unsought fecundity, amid children's howling and distributing clips round the ear, all the while standing in a draught with her thin skirt clinging round her knees and an infant sucking at the edge of a dirty cardigan at one moment and at the exhausted bare breast at another, this mother refused to send a single one of her spirited, hungry band into exile.

Among these desperate families in their death throes in now subdued Schiffbek, there is one so happy that women neighbours come round in the evenings to listen to its unusual tranquillity. A small, dark woman, prematurely aged but with the blackest eyes and the duskiest colouring and something southern about her voice that crackles like well-baked ash-covered chestnuts snapping under the embers in the frost. Her children, four of them, are as if planned, either quite blond with blue eyes or olive-skinned with black eyes. Little Czechs and little Germans alternately. Her husband is comrade R., an old communist who had been beaten up in the army because of his Polish surname and his dangerously taciturn manner behind which the sergeant-major sensed a pacifist; a member of the Spartacus Group, one of the oldest fighters in the KPD and wounded in the Kapp Putsch.

There are periods in every man's life when pus accumulates and festers. Every abrasion — baby's sickness, an unpleasant exchange with the boss, meeting a spy just after coming out of an illegal gathering — all take a nasty, malignant turn. Comrade R., a foreigner and burdened with a family, out of work half the week and long known as a communist, felt keenly that he and his four could at any minute now slip under the wheel. They were all very tired, growing terribly hungry and cold.

Then the battles. Yet October had not yielded the victory which Schiffbek, that Verdun of the Hamburg Rising, had so fantastically believed in. The police had not managed to catch R. who had taken such an energetic part in the movement.

From abroad he sent his wife a letter and a visa. One of those rare miracles that still do happen.

Everyone in R.'s flat thawed out, relaxed, took a breath and started to talk in undertones.

That letter from abroad was like the scrape of a distant spade digging those five human beings out of the avalanche that had crashed on to their roof.

Hamm

The Hamm quarter. This district is highly inconvenient for street fighting because of the lay-out of its broad straight streets.

It is difficult to tie its expansive avenues in a girdle of barricades. The smooth, bare frontages of the workers' barracks fall sheer to the slippery asphalt. The walls provide no cover for lone marksmen who prefer the ledges, bays and lofty porchways of the older-style dwellings. Spades and crowbars break their teeth trying to dig up that rolled-out lava. You need to fell a few fully-grown trees to seal off such a street. But trees do not grow in slum quarters. What's more Hamm's straight, empty, smooth streets like stone channels, can easily be defended by one machine-gun mounted at a cross-roads: there are miles of exposed spaces that mercilessly betray to binoculars any crouching figure, in vain seeking cover and protection in the mean shadow of those inhuman façades — a figure with a cap pulled down over his eyes, a woollen scarf wound round his chin and a rifle in his hands.

All these unfavourable features did not prevent Hamm from becoming the arena of brief but very intense battles. Not even the motley petty-bourgeois nature of the population could dull them: to a man the students that made up a considerable proportion of it offered their services to the police — not on their home ground but after they had stolen off to more secure sectors of the city.

98

An armed rising presupposes the presence of people with weapons in their possession. The Hamburg Rising was a rising of unarmed workers confronted above all with arming themselves at the expense of the enemy.

In the Hamm zone there were five police stations permanently occupied by Sipo units; apart from the weapons in the hands of the policemen the military organisation was expecting to seize the small armouries in each one.

Thus in Hamm as in other parts of the city the struggle started with unarmed workers seizing the small police fortresses guarded by sentries and packed with their military complement and ammunition of every kind.

One of the toughest police stations was seized by twelve workers with an antiquated pistol.

At the very doorway of the police station the detachment seemed to waver. Then one of the comrades whose name, Rolf-shagen, can be spoken with pride — the gates of a hard-labour camp have now slammed behind him — tossed out to his men: *"Nun man los!"* (Well, let's go!) and, without looking to see if anyone was following or not, leapt over the three steps with his huge legs and burst into the station. Behind him came his friend, a young compositor, but no one else. The only revolver, unloaded at that, was jabbed into the crowd of Sipos. Seeing their indecision, Rolfshagen bellowed in a quite unreal voice and crashed his fist down meaningfully on the table. Papers started to fly, the holy oil in the inkwells was spattered about and state power tottered to its foundations.

"Man los, hier wird nicht lange gefackelt!" (Let's go, it's no time to hang about!)

The police surrendered, put their hands up and were disarmed and locked away by the comrades who had caught them up. What should they do now? Hold out in the captured *Revier* (police station) or go out on to the streets and dig in, or rush to the aid of Barmbeck from where the sound of relentless gunfire reached their ears? And all the while there was no contact with the centre.

When sitting in his corner at party meetings, sucking on

his pipe silently fluffing himself up in his bristly hunched water-proof docker's gear, Rolfshagen would never chatter. He did not like phrases, silver as bicycle-wheel spokes, and the calls to struggle of which party intellectuals are so fond. He conceived of an uprising as something simple and straightforward, without retreats, without the slightest vacillations and deviations, like the sweep of a crane snatching up its prey, the straightness of a compass needle and the unerring course of a ship. And so, without receiving any instructions, Rolfshagen loaded his rifle, stacked up the cartridges in handy piles and made ready to fight it out and die beside a window whose ledge afforded a slight cover.

His comrades tried in vain to draw him along with them, arguing the whole danger of a position that could be surrounded and cut off. Rolf decided to stay.

"Dat is Befehl ick blieb" (That's an order, I'm sticking to it) and he stayed. An hour later this man's duel with the police who had flooded into the district began. Having fired his last cartridge he finally fell, wounded in the head, chest and stomach, losing consciousness from a terrific boot to the ribs.

Rolfshagen did not die in the hospital where they had removed six pieces of lead from his body. Confident of the revolution's speedy victory he refused to run but with a grin accepted the ten years' hard labour which Scheidemann's 'mercy' had granted him. Even in the doorway of the court he turned round to the crowd and shouted to his friends interspersed among the thick wad of bourgeois in the audience:

"Don't forget to keep my revolver clean; I'll be coming out to get it soon!"

That was the capture of the Fort Street police station.

Now, Mittelstrasse. To begin with, Charli Setter, a member of the provincial parliament who had been entrusted with the leadership of a combat unit, did not show up until right at the very end of the conflict and displayed a shameful lack of resolution, diffidence and faintheartedness.

Secondly, a worker, no longer young but extremely agile and, as they say in German, *aufgeweckt,* whose narrow anaemic face was framed by a small black beard like a black-edged mourning envelope and twitched with the vague tremble of neuralgic pain. He had sat out the entire war in the trenches and came out a cripple, gravely wounded in the head, susceptible to agonising pains, epileptic fits and hysteria. His disability had not however stopped his injured head from re-considering and reviewing his old convictions as a social democrat and party official. Cursing the war and the workers' party that had acted as its livestock supplier he courageously broke with the organisation he had belonged to for over fifteen years.

The comrades were afraid to rely too much upon K. whom simple party discussions had caused to recant. But during the *Aktion* he not only remained in the battles and risked the greatest danger but never gave free rein to his fractured nerves. His conduct was irreproachable from start to finish.

In the assault on police station no. 23 two remarkable brothers marched alongisde K. Rott, a curly-headed giant and building worker by trade. I cannot remember the exact description of his *Branche* (trade). Anyway it was a short tradesman's formula that included iron, concrete and coal. It had a proud ring like the motto on an order of labour. In reply to all my questions this comrade merely shook his Siegfriedian head and refused at any price to disclose any information about his personal role in the business. So a long shadow continues to lie across that stern regular face: one like those of the caryatides dumbly holding up a whole structure. Beside him was L., a highly-skilled joiner and a man of exceptional culture and courage. The swarthy colour of his face, the southern vivacity of his eyes and the mock romanticism with which he defaces and gouges out the planed, lacquered commonplaces of political jargon (just as the craftsman tests the blade of his tool on the edge of his bench), seem to point to Slav and possibly Jewish blood. A fiery political temperament and a cool inward sobriety thanks to which L., as one of the finest and most remarkable Hamburg fighters, never for one instant forgets deep within himself that the revolution's most flaming words are in fact written in crude oil paint on cheap red calico. An enthusiast with a small, hermetically-sealed ice-box in his heart. His conscious self-abnegation and the fury with which he can at the requisite moments cast aside the cool rationality which bugged him, are far more valuable than any innate valour.

Three anarchist brothers fought alongisde Rott and L. Brave men who had left the party a few months earlier because of its inactivity, but who took up rifles as soon as the password for the Rising was issued. Their whole family consists of communists. The sixty-year-old mother, the sisters and the two brothers-in-law also took part in the movement. In short, a family cell, a Soviet knot of which there are quite a few deep down among German workers. This group (twenty-eight workers with two revolvers and one rubber truncheon) overran their police station quite brilliantly, surrounding it on either side, disarming the police and availing themselves of its store of arms.

Meanwhile, around seven o'clock, day began to break. Street traffic had come to a halt (to be sure, only for a few hours in this part of the city) and detachments of armed workers stopped their workmates who were going off to work without suspecting a thing and sent them home.

"What's happened?"

"The dictatorship of the proletariat has been declared."

"Dat kun jo sen, ook io nich wieder gohn. (Maybe, but it won't last.)

"Dan got wi werra nochüs." (Then let's go home.)

Not to the barricades, not to the aid of the workers' hundreds but home.

Very typical too.

In spite of the lack of further orders from the Staff Centre the majority of insurgents quit the ravaged police stations and moved off in the direction of smoke-shrouded Barmbeck where frantic shooting would not cease. The only sensible tactic had been arrived at by instinct. There was no way of lifting the asphalt. There were almost no trees. There were too few weapons for them to bring in wider masses; therefore the armed groups dispersed in different directions so as to percolate individually to the embattled quarters.

Rott, L. and the anarchist brothers' detachment (nine rifles and twelve revolvers altogether) proceeded in the direction of the heaviest exchanges. In one of the stone corridors they were peppered with machine-gun fire from a lorry. The riflemen threw themselves to the ground and then under the canopy of ever closer fire took cover down a side street. One of the comrades dropped down on one knee and raised his rifle to his shoulder. It fell instantly from his hands. L. recalls a stream of blood trickling from the pavement, washing into the gutter a cigarette-end someone had dropped. From one side came the roar of a second vehicle. Not noticing the partisans it stood self-assuredly across the end of a small street its heavy undefended flank facing down it. The insurrectionaries fairly swept it with carbine fire. Then the little detachment adopted a mobile square formation switching from place to place for many hours, finally giving real battle on the Central Canal bridge. It was a collapsible, sprawling square which, at the required moment, would roll up and disappear like water on sand. In the centre, three or four first-rate marksmen. They occupy an intersection or the main junction of several major streets. On every adjacent corner look-outs armed with revolvers are posted, each covered by a newspaper kiosk, telephone box or tree-trunk. They fire only at close range during hand-to-hand skirmishes and warn the carbineers of an imminent encirclement. Dashing from place to place, defending and surrendering successive nodal points, this flying squad of marksmen eventually consolidates by the bridge over the Central Canal where the stone creases of the surrounding streets converge in a broad fan. The bridge gently arches its broad back in order to step primly over the course of a wan, ebbing factory canal that is like a thorn in its flesh. The marksmen lie down so that only the barrels of their rifles protrude over the bridge's hump. Growing up in corsets of iron rods much thicker than their own trunks are a few miserable trees that have not fled this spot only because the concrete has squeezed their sapling roots into clods; they and an emaciated lamp-post provide the only cover for the combatants set out to the right and left of the three sharpest-shooting hunters.

All along the bank uninhabitable buildings drop murkily

into the water. Only occasionally does a cellar peep-hole open up in a wall spread through with damp. It looks like a shivering gaping mouth surfacing to take a gulp of air only to disappear once again. This is a working-class Venice; where palaces of cotton, fat and iron have no wide marble staircases and embankments; where brick and concrete lapped by poisonous sewage is covered with deposits of regal beauty, coatings of pale green, grey and pinky-brown tints more whimsical and varied than porphyry, marble and malachite — the blood, pearl and ash of the high Quattrocento. The grandeur of the craggy cul-de-sacs is underlined not by time but glistening coal. Its shadows are more tragic than those Tintoretto's hand painted for blossoming Venice. This lagoon that washes round industrial Hamburg knows neither gondolas nor romantic nights. It carries out to sea factory waste, dampness, cold and all the diseases that soak through the walls into the life, dreams, labour and blood of millions of workers. Like doges the factory chimneys look at themselves in cloudy mirrors. Smoke drifts down from their shoulders like resplendent robes and they are betrothed to their grey, cold, polluted sea not by the gold ring of the Adriatic but by the wail of ships' sirens heralding the arrival of precious raw materials. The nereids have long ago died off in the cold filth of the canals. Now and again urchins fish out of the water the white corpse of a fish floating belly upwards with painfully distended gills.

Over this canal they fought it out. Suddenly the look-outs reported vehicles. They had to change position again. Marksmen once more in the middle of the square and scouts on the corners. A lorry packed with soldiers flies unexpectedly round a corner. With one well-aimed shot Rott manages to damage the engine. The Sipos abandon their vehicle and carry off their wounded. The detachment again makes a desperate sprint and occupies the hub of the next quarter. This time it is attacked by an armoured car under cover of which a line of Greens spreads out. The partisans pick off the lieutenant — a plucky but stupid lieutenant who had sprung forward courageously to rally his men for the assault at the top of his voice. Panic among the Sipos succeeded by a numbing stillness;

a stillness quite appropriate to that ghostly realm of deserted canals picked out by the silently fluttering banners of factory smoke and the far-off salvos of the Rising being quelled.

The insurgents continue to advance along empty streets, by motionless, glassy rivers, past idle factories locked up like monasteries and eyeless houses with mouths hostilely shut tight; at crossroads they break their formation that was as light and convenient as a nomad's tent. Finally amid an utter absence of life the rumble of wheels came again across the dead roadway. This time, though, it was only a loaded newspaper truck. Forgetting danger, they fumbled with the tightly lashed bundles and then looked through *Fremdenblatt's* soft pages nowhere finding the only words that throughout that day they had been expecting with more tension and torment than their own victory: news of the revolution throughout Germany and the new Republic of Soviets. Rott screwed up one paper and grabbed another. L. read it and went white. Otto wrapped up his wounded hand in that dirty rag refusing to believe its reports and contemptuously nodding his head. It was lying. Yes, it was deliberately keeping quiet about the victorious rising in Berlin, Saxony and everywhere else. It couldn't be otherwise.

Then they threw the bundles down on to the asphalt and set fire to them. The wind snatched up the blazing sheets and carried them off into the canal. There they drifted like flaming birds, swans set alight.

Volleys crackled in nearby streets. The detachment retreated slowly, illuminated by the ruddy glow of the enormous bonfire that the soldiers were trying in vain to stamp out and break up with their rifle-butts.

Postscript:
German Mensheviks
After the Rising

During the recent rising in Hamburg the dockworkers, who had already been on strike for several days, did not join forces with the fighting masses. They roamed the streets, hands thrust in pockets and with innocent curiosity questioned comrades returning from the districts under police siege: what's up and why? Thousands of workers organised by the social democrats remained peaceful spectators of the Hamburg events. The port workers (with the exception of the shipyards and plants processing petroleum waste, where earnings have fallen to ridiculous levels) are aristocrats compared to the mass of the Hamburg proletariat.

They receive more than the highest grade of inland worker, like, for example, building workers, engineering workers or railwaymen, and of course several times more than those pariahs of Hamburg port, the men employed in the shipyards. During the war this contented layer worked zealously for the war department earning excellent rates of pay; they were exempted from military service and entered the revolution as a cold, reactionary current, perfectly combining their flabby, cosy, contented, petty-bourgeois way of life with an innocuous SPD card. In 1918 this Menshevik-organised mass of well-to-do workers fought might and main against the Council of Workers' Deputies (Soviet), wishy-washy and ambivalent as its policy was. To the demonstrations of unemployed, the banning of bourgeois newspapers and the wrecking of the SPD rag, *The Hamburg Echo,* which had splashed its yellow pages with daily slanders against the Soviet, these workers had replied with a powerful reactionary counter-demonstration, the arrest of the Soviet's chairman, the restoration of the bourgeois Senate and a railwayman's strike that prevented the despatch of strong volunteer units mobilised by the Hamburg proletariat to aid the city of Bremen under siege by General Herstenberg's officer division. In short it was not the first time that dockers and other workers in the countless port warehouses rendered valuable service to the German counter-revolution.

And well they might! From throughout the world merchant vessels converge upon Hamburg's convenient harbour. Shipowners have no time to wait, nor time to haggle about a few irrelevant pfennigs. For every day's delay they have to pay demurrage; delivery dates cannot wait; agreed freightages and rail charges lapse. Due to all these circumstances the stevedores and warehousemen enjoy unquestionable economic privileges while other categories have long since lost both — the eight-hour day and half their pre-war wage! In the course of the revolution's first two years the reactionary influence of the port never ceased to make itself felt. It was against the socialisation of industrial undertakings, the restriction of private commerce and any social turmoil that might weaken the Free City's credit-worthiness abroad, strengthen its foreign competitors and de-populate a port that lives on the ebb and flow of the world market.

Back in 1919 Hamburg Mensheviks imagined that Britain would spare the capital of the *Uferland* (coastal region) in return for their righteous suppression of communism. Today nothing remains of such hopes. The Entente has concertedly chewed up the left-overs of bourgeois-socialist Germany and utterly ruined not just the communists but the most moderate Mensheviks too. Their well-being has faltered, their trade unions gather in alms and their leaders, now chucked out of the Grand Coalition, vote for the dictatorship of the bourgeoisie — yet old traditions die hard. The port has been pauperised, but still it is the best-fed of paupers, and fed without painful interruptions. The grateful labour aristocracy assists the police in clearing away the barricades and visits SPD meetings and rallies *en masse.*

Yesterday was a field-day for them. The Free City of Hamburg was honoured with a visit from the eminent Berliner, the editor of *Vorwärts,* Genosse Stampfer. Hundreds of workers came to listen. Possibly not a single Russian worker would have the patience to read through to the end an article detailing all the distortions of marxist thought that the experienced Menshevik had the temerity to put before a working-class audience; in a city, what is more, where trenches that had criss-crossed the suburbs in every direction had only just been filled in, where tenements in working-class quarters are lacerated with bullets, where dead policemen number dozens and injured, arrested and beaten workers hundreds. And yet you must have a clear conception of the entire decay and headlong decline of working-class and petty-bourgeois Germany, corrupted by half a century of castrated, emasculated pseudo-socialism, to appreciate the tremendous act of heroism that, under such conditions, Hamburg's armed uprising represented. To rise up in that swamp, that cowardly, deeply-reactionary quagmire, was a thousand times harder than beneath our old Tsarist soldier's boot or against a distinct, easily recognisable, renegade black Fascist shirt.

Doctor Stampfer was not trying to be particularly logical. After all he felt himself to be in the provinces where a good player can without embarrassment cheat with a clearly marked card. In the first place all Germany's misfortunes stem from the endless multiplicity of regional parliaments. They should be abolished and centralised. Secondly, only a strong state power is capable of protecting the working class from the offensive of capital. Only the state (shouts: 'what sort?' 'bourgeois?') can uphold the eight-hour day for the workers. Even worthy, portly, greying SPD members started to feel ill at ease somehow, but German Mensheviks have the orator's ingenuous and always effective remedy: as soon as the gallery begins to whistle and the old men start looking round at each other restively and mutter: 'Oh, yes? Well I never!', the speaker drags Wilhelm out on to the stage. Alive, in moustache and full military dress. The speaker need only punch him on the nose, tell a couple of anecdotes about the ex-emperor's stupidity and have the unprecedented courage to abuse Wilhelm as a fool, idiot and maniac for the philistine to quake rapturously in the face of such blasphemy and the audience to be conquered. Having spat at Wilhelm the SPDer passes on to the communists.

It turns out that it is they who have smashed the sacred chalice of the Republic. Lacking any esteem for the legal forms of democracy and the noble philanthropic methods of parliamentary struggle they have sullied the skirts of that innocent maiden, the Republic, with the blood of their own brother proletarians.

Amid a deep hush Stampfer hurls his accusation:

"In Prussia communists brutally tortured two police officers. Isn't the poor *Schupo* (policeman) as much a proletarian as ourselves?"

From somewhere above a very shrill mocking wail stifled by virtuous grunting:

"Down with Scheidemann! Hang Ebert from the lamppost!"

"Ebert," says the *Vorwärts* editor beating his starched breast, "Ebert, that son of the people, has attained the supreme responsibilities of state thanks to his talents! The German proletariat can be proud that a son from its own depths has reached such a peak!"

Pope Ebert appears aloft in the clouds of parliamentarism. The Republic stretches forth over him the crown of victory, and signals to the ballot box: one out of millions can win two hundred thousand pounds or become president. Democracy's divine lottery.

Stampfer admits to some of the party's mistakes with a disarming frankness. The party has been learning. Nothing is gained without trials and suffering. "But why do we always only condemn our own party — it debilitates us. We should make our criticisms in private, face to face. Take, for example, Dr. Hertz, Breitscheid and myself." A note of confidence and intimate simplicity. "They voted against the motion of confidence in the

Marx government but I was for it. So what? Did we quarrel over it? You just don't! We travelled in the same compartment and didn't talk politics — we were up to here with it (a gesture of having had his fill) and on the station we had some sausages together. But think how we had argued about it in the faction — almost coming to blows."

The electors are always flattered when they are allowed to take a peep through the keyhole into the kitchen of big-time politics. Ten or twelve speakers, one after another, spoke against the worthy *Vorwärts*. They demonstrated the following elementary truths: 1) the social democrats have safely delivered the dictatorship of the bourgeoisie; 2) such a dictatorship will be directed exclusively against the working class; 3) the SPD bears not only moral but also formal responsibility for this.

All those speakers who, in their ten allotted, fast-flowing minutes punctuated by the chairman's bell, attempted tortuously to substantiate their most profound disillusionment with the party and their rage at its crimes were met with clapping, nodding and loud pre-arranged ovations. Then, with exceptional uniformity and an overwhelming majority, a motion of confidence in the SPD's parliamentary faction was carried. Having given their deputy a chewing-over, shoved his nose in the sins of the SPDers and revealed their complete understanding of his sharkish tricks, the electors wiped Stampfer's broken nose clean and let him go off home with a vote of full confidence. A card-sharp must not dupe his own side for then he will be beaten. But cheat for the benefit of that dear middle class and outplay the hated revolution — he can and should.

In Hindenburg's Country

Preface to
the German Edition

I have travelled through Germany, 'Hindenburg's country', and seen it with the unclouded eyes of a visitor from the country of workers and peasants, Lenin's country. You have castles and museums, government palaces where ministers sit, victory avenues and victory monuments, madhouses, war memorials, barracks, schools, prisons and factories — millions of people sucked dry and a bourgeoisie with culture, technology and all the comforts of a good life.

But I did not merely wish to learn about German streets and who was begging, starving, strolling, motoring or parading in them, but rather to see the places from where it is all being invisibly ruled and where the millions of threads and cables come together: the power centres of public opinion and the industrial workshops of the German spirit, German culture and German guns.

I have looked for Germany within her *national sanctuaries.*

Krupp and Essen

The cities of the Ruhr with their streets, plants and pits are marked with the name of Krupp just like the teaspoons and pillowslips of a propertied family. Essen is but a hereditary estate, a family possession passed down from generation to generation. The family, as if in its own home, casually puts up memorials to its deceased members in the public squares and gardens. Grandma orders one monument, the cousins or sons or grandsons who have tastes and pleasures of their own, another. At every junction, a bronze Friedrich-Albrecht, an Albrecht-Franz or a Franz-Friedrich. The buildings, tramlines, people and vehicles meekly give way to their iron masters. The cult of ancestors reigns over the greatest of Europe's industrial centres. The last male of the reigning family died long ago and the outrageous scandal that accompanied him to the grave has long since been forgotten. The daughters, widows unknown to anyone, have inherited thousands of millions by right of blood and become the autocratic sovereigns of hundreds of factories, pits, shipyards, railways and harbours; they are given husbands for the continuance of the line and petty officials turned prince-regents adopt their wives' name and multiply so that the great city of Essen shall not be left without thoroughbred masters, and hundreds of thousands of workers with millions of machines can quietly settle to work for real, pure-blooded little Krupps. Life, of course, has long since outgrown the patriarchal economic forms with which old Adolf started half a century ago; business is managed by the board of a joint-stock company instead of a monarchical lord and the Krupp colossus strides out in a direction fixed and ultimately guided by an army of expert officials rather than by the will of the brilliant organiser and builder that Krupp II had been.

On the site of the city of Essen thirty or forty years ago — where today the giants of metallurgy work so closely crowded together; where plants jostle each other and factory chimneys crane their necks so as not to lose sight of each other partitioning the soot-black sky with thick strips of smoke; where far beneath the city's feet pits gnaw at every piece of coal (between them black covered ways are stretched like cables: each colliery grabs them with a hundred hands and pulls them over to its side); where the great smelting furnaces that knit the Ruhr cities into the body of one gigantic plant are never extinguished — on the site of this Essen were once open fields and scattered peasant farmsteads. You can still see today how the city has grown up from a mine. Concrete and asphalt have merely overlaid its age-old disorder. Streets have formalised the winding, crooked paths trodden by the first miners between pub and works. The city has reconciled itself to wild ungainly houses that will not recognise any discipline. Like tramps turned millionaires overnight they loaf around with pipes between their teeth, without gardens (or without trousers), with the wind blowing freely across their bare stone chests. The city, crushed down with wealth and overcome with the smell of money, rushes on its way pretending that there is nothing here and building bridges to avoid those feet in rough miner's boots stretched out across the street. Essen has from that time onwards retained a passion for reconstruction and large useless earthworks. It loves to sit down and sort through its bag of odds and ends, its old kit-bag. To pull forty-pound stones out of the road surface, dig over the soil so that the stench of bare earth that has not removed its

stone shirt for decades hangs over the city and then put everything
back in place, open a tramline and light up street-lamps. The city,
like the web of a goose's foot, lies mostly between the works. Its
dwelling-houses are squeezed in between the factory blocks,
huddling against the fences and afraid to be the first to take a single
patch of vacant land without permission from the coal syndicate.
Any narrow multi-familied back-street has only to take a run
forward to find at its end a factory chimney standing like a
watchman waving a smoky flag:

"Go back, this is Rhine Steel" or "this is Herkules" or "this
is AEG".

So the very smallest houses have such a cramped look and
bulging eyes. Black, half-blind, round-shouldered and capped with
tiny roofs they cling to the walls of banks, plants and commercial
offices. They are pits full of people which creep upwards because
the terrible pressure is forcing them up from the ground.

All the plants in Essen city belong to Krupp and all its
housing is the property of Stinnes. The ineffable squalour of the
latter was until recently still entered as an asset in that concern's
fabulous accounts.

But even where factories are compelled to move aside to let
streets and tramlines through the fissures they still remain
masters; the alleyways are so narrow that women could dry their
washing on lines thrown across from one window to another. But
instead, the works has stretched its own cables, pipes and bridges
across the pavements. It strides over the roofs and blocks of flats
like a giant across Lilliputian cottages. Quite unashamed, this lord
and master: it ejects its waste directly on to the street, spitting
steam, ash, water and grime on to the heads of passers-by. Every
one rushing past the wide-open windows can see it beating its
constant wife, pliant but unyielding steel, with a hammer. Children
in their beds are awakened by her screeching and shrieking. Day
and night the dormitories that hug the factories hear iron crying
out like an infant in pain. Every object in workers' homes shudders

like an anvil — even though the blows are falling far away — and adjusts its breathing to those sighs borne on the wind. The worker unconsciously puts his heart and his watch — a silver miner's watch like an onion and with a fat black hand like a finger — forward or back so as to be right by the works' hooter. Everything keeps the same time. Hundreds of thousands, an army of miners and metalworkers, move about, sleep, work, wake up and have their dinner without missing the pace, falling out of the column or breaking their march and never, even in the moments of deepest oblivion, cease to hear that martial music of labour issuing from the factories on to the city, its outskirts and the whole workpeople.

In all Essen there is only one spot where deep solemn stillness reigns. And that is not by any means the so-called 'estates' for the works long ago caught them up, swallowing them whole with their flower-beds and the bees that died from the coal-dust. Nor is it the country club where a speck of nature with grass, leaves and a fishing-pond has been specially set aside for loyal office-workers and their children. (This club looks at everything with one eye, screwing the other tightly up and turning away so as not to see the factory chimneys that waft their dirty clouds of smoke even here, to this garden of delights for sixth-grade officials.) No, real stillness, one so deep that not even the best lift gliding down past every floor can plumb its depths, stillness insulated and shut off from the outside world by glass walls of silence, is in the main office and board room of the Krupp works. Not an office but, strictly speaking, a ministry. Not a board but a government. Oak, leather and halls as if for coronations. The portraits of kings are only incidental. In places of far greater honour are guns with their wives and godmothers; samples of steel and certificates awarded at international exhibitions. Something about the whole of it — those expanses of officialdom, the deep pools of secrecy and staid respectability — is more appropriate to both the Quai d'Orsay and the Foreign Office, or, in Petersburg, the old embankment or the gloomy house by the canal where the Reichswehr mission is today. Applicants who have gulped that atmosphere fall lifeless into the armchairs. Nearly everyone, even specialist technicians with top references, go away without achieving anything. Krupp has a crisis so Krupp has the pick. The firm's internal life is known to very few. Even his own people make mistakes.

"May I see Major von R.?"

The old functionary answers with a grin:

"You mean Colonel von R.?"

"What, since only last year?"

"Yes, Mr. Consul . . ."

They continue to move up the ladder of ranks that is not supposed to have existed after 9 November. They walk in single file or overtake each other in the slow promotion race while in the shadows someone shifts its faithful servants from one step to the next. Second lieutenants become lieutenants; lieutenants, captains; captains, majors. Quite young men take up the vacant posts in this force without fighting men, this army without lower ranks.

His own General Staff so, naturally, his own diplomatic corps. Over recent years it has shrivelled in size and been sharply reduced. The cannon king recalled his ambassadors long ago. Today they sit around the small houses built by Madame Krupp for her old domestic retinue, receiving tiny salaries and eating herring-tails with the daintiest family silver, while in drawing rooms where the crown prince's horsey face with its pair of bubbles under the eyes looks on they reminisce about the days when one word from the Krupp representative in Peking meant more than all the assurances of official envoys. Yuan Shih-kai would pay regular trips to a little Chinese house far from the hated European quarter where he would purchase advice and order guns. Then came the war — and all was lost! Yet to this day what sources of information and what contacts Krupp has! In the *Essener Zeitung* brief items on foreign and, particularly, eastern affairs are indicative of a vast operation that is quietly in hand. While the Foreign Ministry gropes to find a route for German exports, here in Essen they have long understood what a Chinese market can mean for German industry. Her revolutionary struggle is followed with the closest attention, prices offered, relations renewed; they watch and they wait. I happened to get into an argument about China with one of the Krupp managers. To add the final telling weight to his argument he snatched open a desk drawer with an impatient motion, unfolded a fresh report and revealed first odd lines and then odd pages — it was a résumé of every movement and every word of Comrade Karakhan in Peking!

The rectangular tower on the roof of the main administrative block has outgrown all the other factory buildings on its skyward path, outreaching the sharp pinnacles of an old monastery that laboriously sends up to heaven its peals and laments about the machines whose constant vibration crumbles the church walls: 'O Lord, who shall come unto my fourth-century Christ with beads of sweat on his brow when a 25,000-ton blast furnace is smoking next door? O Lord, grant that this be not so!' But Essen's heaven has changed. It is just the cloudy vault of a railway station, the ceiling of an immense factory. Where the glass panes have been smashed you can see a bit of blue. But high up there a celestial ventilator quickly slams it out again.

A lift cuts a thick slice off the house of Krupp like a razor. First the applicants are left behind, then the lower floors fall away and finally, in the building's head, the corridors are grey and still like the coils of a brain. A young girl with a yellow complexion who drops up and down in her box for ten hours a day pushes the door back. How strange. Here is a dining-room set for ten people, as bright as a lighthouse around which the whistling wind lashes rain and soot against walls of glass. "Here", our escort whispers, a former officer with a scar-like mouth and a black glove on his wooden hand, "here the demigods dine".

Sitting at the table you can see Essen and all Krupp's kingdom. The history of German imperialism written out in lines of factory blocks with chimneys as punctuation marks. All around the horizon is scribbled over with them like notes in the margin of a ledger. Like a stock-jobber, the wind rubs them off the sky's board every minute and washes it down with a rainy sponge to write up new signs and figures. The smoke creeps up in long erratic lines as if representing the level of Krupp's yearly dividends. The sky is playing the stock-exchange, the sky is buying and selling.

Far below amid concrete and granite is the little wooden house with two windows where the first Krupp set to work a hundred years ago. He had wanted to take advantage of the weak state of British industry during the Latin American Wars of Independence and forge a powerful rival upon German anvils but lost all his fortune, was ruined and died in the little house while British steel ruled the world market undefeated. The crisis had ended too soon, the German bourgeoisie was still in nappies and its prophet who lacked both credit and cash was crushed together with his experiments and his one blast furnace. His son started from the beginning. For twenty-five years he worked to prepare steel's victory over iron. The victory of the steel gun cast in one piece over the old bronze cannon. He sent a top-quality steel ingot weighing 2,000 kilos to the London Exhibition of 1851. That lump, which gained a gold medal, was a warning that no one understood. It was destined twenty years later to flatten the French war industry. Within that ingot, before which the thousands of visitors had stood in ecstasy, was Sedan.

On the eve of the Franco-German War a prototype of the modern steel gun was already complete. Krupp had become a world name. Short and cast in one piece like his steel it boomed out first in Europe and then in Asia. It was uttered wherever thunder-clouds gathered. 'Krupp' meant 'war'. A new war whose horrors were still unknown to mankind, a new mode of death and a new strategy unlike those before. On the Ruhr, over in the west of Germany, all day and night plants smoked, furnaces blazed and the metal poured and cast to produce heavy guns, rifles, mortars, howitzers and explosive devices for anyone who could pay. It was the arsenal of the world.

Krupp was born a German and a patriot, in so far as any businessman can be a patriot of one country. That meant that the

German Kaiser would be received at the Krupp court more frequently and informally than others seeking his friendship. Any new invention would be offered first to him. The fatherland was the first among customers. But if the fatherland could not pay or requested a deferment the goods would pass into enemies' hands. Pinner writes: 'In the days when Krupp threw the barrels of his guns on to the market for the first time, nobody was tormented with pangs of conscience or prejudices of a political nature. Everyone would without hesitation sell his instruments of murder to both friends and foes. Bismarck's wars were but a proving ground, the ordeal by fire, for his guns.'

Had the French government realised the superiority of Krupp's guns and hastened to re-equip its army the war of 1870 might well have ended differently.

The subsequent forty years were the period of the coming of age of German industry and its imperialism. Krupp turned into a whole state. He was one of the first to reconstruct his whole industrial process in the form of the vertical trust. Everything from coal-mines to engineering plants, from ore deposits to power stations. Everything at first hand, everything his own product. He made his rear secure and waged war against middlemen and whole alliances of middlemen for the independence of the raw material: ore, fuel and chemicals. His furnaces, plants and workshops acquired their own foreign colonies. Krupp conquered for them whole territories and seas of oil. He strangled his neighbours like chickens, swallowing up their assets or forcibly merging them with his own in the form of joint-stock companies.

On the very eve of the war, in 1913 probably, Krupp uttered a brilliant remark at a press banquet which passed as unnoticed as that lump of steel sixty years before:

"A factory must create its own demand."

Krupp made guns and war was his customer. In 1914 it broke out.

Never had the works flourished as it did in the first years of the war. 130,000 workers were employed in armaments manufacture. 40,000 would sit down at a time to eat in the factories.

The old buildings were finished and new ones shot up at an incredible speed. Taking the first year of the war alone the firm's turnover rose from 33.9 million gold marks in 1913 to 86.4 million in 1914. Finally, on the outskirts where nowadays French soldiers have their firing practice and sing those merry songs, there grew a flat-roofed lizard, a dark red barn beneath which the earth shook night and day. The greatest gun plant in Europe. This, the Hindenburg Works, had arisen thanks to that celebrated plan for the militarisation of industry whose father the Field Marshal was considered to be. Simple, this plan: flood heavy industry with gold and cram the country's last resources into its maw but force it to turn out more guns than all the allies' plants put together. Krupp was beaten at this game. Vickers-Armstrong and the Bethlehem Steel Corporation proved the stronger. Today, the day the Hindenburg programme was implemented is regarded as the day of the German mark's final decline, the beginning of the fall and the beginning of the inflationary years.

No one had been so enriched by the war as Krupp. No one was dealt such a blow by the Versailles Peace as he. The machines that had produced the arms were blown up. Tools in the shell shops were wrecked or removed. Whole districts fell silent and dozens of chimneys stopped smoking. The pits and mines in Alsace, Luxembourg and the Saar passed mostly into the hands of French industrialists who treated them exactly as Krupp would have done in the event of victory. The sites of the now destroyed or paralysed installations have become yawning gaps. Fresh reserves of the raw materials, lost for ever at home across the Rhine, had to be found abroad.

Krupp made an attempt to switch over to peacetime rails. Hitherto he had never made *things* in the accepted sense of the word. But now he is largely following his original path: you can't make soup or sew dresses with his products. His plants produce not goods for consumption but the means of production. Krupp is a nursery for pedigree horse power, the breeding-ground for siring machines that will in turn beget countless generations of motors. His looms are like queen-bees from which the life of entire bee-hives springs. Their slim steel bodies toss out millions of feet of cloth and his lorries and cranes shift thousands of tons. Railway wheels are but bobbins around which space is wound. Self-emptying wagons, diesel engines, struts for overhead railways, harvesters and machines for potato-planting and spreading fertilisers. Rakes and mowers, shovels and locomotive boilers, oil storage tanks and pipes — all are embryos of factories, the sperm of new airways and towns and the tonnage of fleets that will carry the crops of the next decades.

Nonetheless there are no trifles for Krupp today. Krupp scorns nothing. He has been forbidden to make guns. All right. He will make false teeth — light, durable, stainless, odourless, tasteless steel jaws. Ten times cheaper than platinum and just as good. He fell upon the dairy maids, took away the rags and strainers through which they used to pour milk into the bottle and gave them lovely separators for twenty marks each. The great Krupp struck up a friendship with the smallest and darkest cinemas where the boss's daughter plays the piano. Now they will buy their projectors only from him. He tempted doormen's wives, little post-office clerks, old maids, schoolteachers and chemists into buying his magic lantern. He supplied thousands of grocers with their cash registers. Yet all these are still trifles, even all this is insufficient to stop the gap. Krupp has been caught off-balance. He must take a new stride forward and carry out a technical revolution if he is to beat the foreign competitor without guns and bayonets.

But there they still are, visible from the tower. At lunch every day the directors count up the dead shells with their eyes: the long flat roofs of the Hindenburg Works; there they lie in the midst of plants with a smell that seems to turn fouler every day like the carcass of a rotting whale. A silent polygon resembling a cemetery. A dead building beneath a dome looking like a dormant, black, Petersburg Admiralty: that's the factory that worked for the navy. There are the endless workshops of the gun plant lying drawn out like a gun's barrel, sealed up on the outside and empty inside with flights of stairs showing through the glass walls like bones through skin. Somewhere there booms not a cannon but a hammer — a hydraulic press is stamping out cisterns and boilers for chemical plants. But this work too will soon come to a halt. Today boilers but tomorrow cannon again. No, it's better all blown up. The Control Commission is implacable.

The engineering plant that suffered so cruelly now works at half capacity and is the largest in Europe occupying an area 47,000 square metres. Its last big order was for locomotives for Russia. But many months have passed since then and Russia is making her own locomotives.

Away to the west are open-hearth furnaces with their clear yards, a square grey lake of water from underground, towers with the racing wheels of winding gear — a few of those pits that are still operating — gasometers, garages for hundreds and thousands of vehicles, a hunchbacked house — the laboratory where a rust-proof iron was discovered this year — steel mills, more open-hearths, blast furnaces, chemical works, textile machinery plants, all fanning outwards. Some of these have been snuffed out, others are half-empty, while yet others are working three shifts flat out, setting world productivity records with the lowest possible wages and the longest possible working day.

From this height it is all quite plain: these plants, factories and workshops are not standing still at all. They are moving and their movements are co-ordinated like on a chessboard or a battle plan. Some edge round their own corpses, stepping over their empty yards and structures, while others, weakened and unable to keep their feet, are assigned to the rear to re-arm and replenish themselves with new energy. The burden is being wholly shifted off their shoulders on to the stronger ones. The latter have to bear double the load as the clouds of smoke hang over Krupp's camp like banners of the armies.

A crisis. Yes. Elsewhere, for the press, creditors and the workers at whose expense the silent technical revolution is being prepared, it is a palace *coup* by machines. But for these latter merely an acute coal crisis. Apparently German coal can no longer compete with British coal. The Ruhr's newspapers are full of the news that Russian coal which no one had taken seriously before, is beating German and British coal in the Balkans and throughout the Near East. Production costs must be brought down otherwise the economy will collapse — that is the catchphrase of all the right-wing, democratic and social-democratic press. And so down with miners' pensions, down with their leave and public holidays, away with national insurance and pit safety legislation and away with all the proletariat's rights gained in a fifty-year battle.

In order to demonstrate the gravity of the crisis to the workers the Krupp family has resolved upon drastic measures. It has dismissed no less than forty footmen from its castle and moved from its palace, which was as large and ugly as a covered market, to a well-appointed town house. The magnanimous gentlemen are sharing their travails honestly with their workers. By saving on the wages of a couple of stable-lads Krupp can throw another few score thousand on to the streets with a clear conscience. Heavy industry's wounded body is convulsively shrinking. It rationalises its production and discards everything superfluous, everything with little or no profitability. Over the last few months some forty thousand men in Essen and the surrounding district alone have been thrown on to the street. Krupp feels no need to conceal the fact that a hundred thousand more will be sacked this winter. The state — that means the taxpayer and that means the worker — will feed these armies of unemployed and their families at its own expense so as to give Krupp and Stinnes a chance to hatch their conspiracy without undue losses: a conspiracy for an uprising of manufacturing industry. Coal — yes, that's what the uprising is directed against. Coal is the black bread of industrial plants which for just over a hundred years has kept the world dependent upon its prices and quality. In order not to be totally overthrown it must adopt a constitution, accept concessions, dissolve itself, turn liquid and share equal rights with the brown coal it had hitherto held in contempt.

The Versailles Treaty exploded and halted half Krupp's works. But it did leave in the hands of the German bourgeoisie its great and inexhaustible source of wealth: that sinewy backbone of Ruhr miners and metalworkers. Krupp, by supporting himself on this spinal column, today makes convulsive attempts to drag himself out of the crisis. Not just to darn holes but to take a new step forward. German social democracy and its trade unions are assisting Krupp's stabilisation as loyally as they had assisted him during the war. For only under their cover can the uprising of the machines be carried out, metallurgy's Ninth of Thermidor.

A Concentration Camp
of Poverty

The Barracks and a Cobbler's Wife

In Germany a man out of work is not threatened with starving to death. The benefit that he receives from the state is, as they say here, too little to live on but too much to die on. An unemployed man will continue to exist on the brink of utter poverty. He has nothing except a piece of dry bread. A family man is in no position to afford a flat, however small, out of this assistance. Once thrown out of his factory he automatically flies from the block, neighbourhood and district where he has lived for many years and where a communist may maintain dangerous contacts. Then the city authority will allocate him accommodation somewhere on the outskirts in an empty abandoned barracks, a regimental stable converted into a hostel or an unoccupied ordnance depot. These are the special concentration camps of poverty: godforsaken stone barns that the Empire had built for the soldiery but which the republic now settles with unreliable workers.

No grass grows on these fields trampled by decades of Prussian drilling. Ragged children play in sewage puddles around the sentry-boxes.

These huge structures that spat entire armies on to the battlefields, stand empty, murky and desecrated. With what bile must the hearts of the former officers who have moved on to the neighbouring Reichswehr barracks be filled when they see a worker's hand-cart, laden with shabby goods and chattels, jingling and trundling in the heat of the day over the field of Mars towards this drab, dismal hermitage.

The wives of the poor folk attach washing-lines to the old eagles on the gates and dry their rags on the sacrosanct window-ledges of the officers' former quarters. A lame red-haired cobbler, now eighteen months out of work 'because of politics' has dragged a soldier's old stove out of the ruined barracks and saws it in half in the sunshine, making ready for a hard winter.

All efforts to make these dead buildings warm and human have been in vain. Objects have been taken from their natural intimacy and spread out, standing heavily to attention along the naked wall. It is impossible to fill barns designed for forty soldiers each with this débris from shipwrecks. The emptiness swallows them up. A bare-footed, bandy-legged child shuffles around on the mucky parquet floor, part of which went for fuel last year when there were not enough panes in the vast and always open windows like eyes without lashes. The second child has died.

Two beds side by side where the father and mother and the boy with his fourteen-year-old sister sleep. A cheerless cur sits in between and yawns.

Every day the communist cobbler's wife washes down the endless corridor out of fear and a desire somehow to appease the hostile house whose walls repeat footsteps and words aloud but without expression. She does this in order to try and come to terms; paying the barracks a pledge of human warmth which the walls accept with as much indifference as a field-marshal accepts a naive bribe from a raw recruit.

But Frau Schumacher need only lift her head to lose her last hope. The old barracks with its dead face repeats from its walls the only words left to it: *"Lerne leiden ohne zu klagen"* Learn to suffer without complaining) or *"Ordnung regiert die Welt"* (order rules the world).

And wherever the poor Frau turns with her bucket and floor-cloth, barrack-room virtue greets her at every step with a fist to her head.

Receiving seven marks a week for four, living on this isle of the dead and knowing that in the evenings in the cramped space her little girl cannot get to sleep for a long time but listens morbidly to every movement and every sigh of her parents — all that's nothing. But hearing that incessant voice from the past prattling with a sluggish tin tongue about valour and obedience, yellow Uhlan uniforms and dashing Hussars who have long ago rotted away somewhere on the Marne or in the Russian snows is just too much.

This winter one more rickety little boy will perhaps no longer be. Perhaps the cobbler himself will pass away for it is hard for him to drag himself along in the rain and cold, damp spells to the labour exchange on his skidding crutches. Yet those spectres will live on and another proletarian family which comes to perish in this unlocked prison where the gates have been ripped from their hinges, where the wind from the field sweeps the crumbling stonework down the corridors and from where there is as little escape as from any other prison, will be greeted by those Fredericuses and the drum-beat of dead bones.

"Furchtlos und treu für Gott, Kaiser und Vaterland." (fearless and true for God, Kaiser and Fatherland) Only one window shines in the dark of the unlit buildings — one gold tooth inside big dead jaws. When it is dark and particularly cold the eagles painted on the ceiling find their way out into the black yard and scratch up the scraps among the rubbish that the cobbler's hens did not manage to peck out.

Into the filthy heaps they dip their pedigree heads adorned with the bald down of the old empire.

Frau Fritzke

Madame Fritzke runs around in stockinged feet so as not to make a noise down those corridors. She is a Ninon de Lenclos of the wastes and on her face love life is packed up in large grey bags.

The atmosphere of this building harms her life: her hair-net, ear-rings and 'Kasan' face-powder all dissolve in it. In the sober light the pipes of her long narrow trousers show horribly clearly through her torn skirt.

Madame Fritzke was widowed during the war. Everyone will sell what they have: since then hundreds have tugged at her breasts, just as the chain is tugged in the lavatory, until they have become long and always seem to be wet. If you were to cut through the lace of her collar they might drop on to the floor and melt away into two large puddles. In this way Frau Fritzke had saved her children from starving to death in the years of the war and inflation. The state that had taken their father from them and spent their orphan's benefit on subsidies to Krupp and Stinnes, has now decided to take them away from their immoral mother. A policeman will arrive in a few days' time and remove the stubborn plump boy and the twelve-year-old girl, an imbecile who has continual fits, to a Catholic orphanage.

August, Frau Fritzke's last friend, had married these relics of love in order to save the family. They had gone along in triumph to the registry office; she, ski-ing over the dust in her narrow lacquered slippers, he in a paper collar reeking of petrol looking as solemn as fate. This heroic measure was the talk of the whole camp but was of no avail.

Fritzke collected together references from her previous employers from which it was clear that she had not only been a prostitute but also a charwoman and that if the morality police gathered up all the filth, muck, soot and cobwebs she had carried out of other people's flats on her back they would have a pyramid in honour of her scorned labour.

But the assessors are adamant. Frau Fritzke weeps. The rings round her eyes are like those drawn with an umbrella in the sand.

An Iron Cross

If you land in the barracks sit down in their depths and don't stir. It's all right for Frau Fritzke to wear her crepe-georgette dress and put special rubber pads on her corns so that they do not break through her shoes but that's her profession.

The cobbler's wife is entitled to heat her curling-irons on the communal stove until her hair — and its nits — crackle, because she married the cobbler (everyone knows this) out of pure love when he was already legless. But nobody else dares raise a comb. Here there is no point in putting on an appearance to impress people with a false idea of your supposed income. Everyone lives in a complete nakedness like snails squashed on the road weakly twitching their horns surmounted by never despairing eyes. So when someone like Mr. Boss is ashamed of his pawnshop receipts and allows no one in his room in case they find out about his feather-bed without a slip and the red pillows out of which the feathers are spurting (which everyone long ago knew about anyway), the affectation is offensive.

In this house, as in paradise or the precinct of a country church, middle-class shame stays behind the gates guarded by the fiery sword of the angel of poverty. If anyone attempts to feel ashamed he at once upsets the others and they too must waste their energies on fig-leaves of pretence which can fool no one. The house, for its part, despises Boss along with the collar on his bare body, the medal on his tummy and that voice sounding as if he'd dined today.

But were it known how much smarting humiliation and bitterness had accumulated right inside those former field-marshal's quarters of his! If anyone had slept on nails and gone grey with hot ashes it was that same Boss who for thirty-four years had worked in a War Department powder-mill.

All his life he was separated from ordinary men by an oath. Men who had taken this soldier's vow of silence entered neither trade union, party nor workingmen's pub. Even reading newspapers of any tendency whatsoever was regarded as improper and suspicious within the gates of the power-mill. What General Staff officers kept quiet about for big money, high ranks, plumed helmets and tiers of decorations on their chests, workers in the powder-mills and munitions plants kept quiet about for nothing, content with the confidence placed in them. That seemed to have turned them from mere hired workers into partners in government. The Kaiser himself was, as it were, indebted to the armaments workers for their modesty and disinterestedness. They loved the dynasty like paupers whose hard-earned pennies a millionaire had deigned to accept from them as credit. And when the war came and gold was smelted into powder and iron, the government actually did do Mr. Boss a great honour by reaching its hand out for his savings book. When that most confidential adviser, the manager's wife, visited his flat with her daughter and servant to offer the old worker a few war-loan bonds, how great was the trepidation and self-sacrifice with which Boss threw all his savings into that abyss!

Ten-pfenning pieces evaporated into thin air like dew. Marks turned to smoke before Boss had time to wipe away his tears of emotion.

As for gold coins — there were 132 of them — no one heard even a slight sound as they fell to the very bottom of the inflation. But Boss was happy.

Since then five, no, more — seven whole years have passed.

The world was drenched in blood, made a convulsive bid to free itself but was finally skinned over with a thin membrane of stabilisation broken by black ice-holes of starvation and unemployment.

When the *Vertiko* (a small cabinet), rocking-chair and clock, received from the works for twenty-five years of irreproachable service, were loaded on to a hand-cart Boss still believed in God and justice.

When his wife came home from the pawnshop with a receipt instead of the personally inscribed silver clock with the imperial monogram, he still held out and did not let her talk at table about their elder son killed in action.

But when all the sacrifices had been offered up and the still patient and devoted Boss began to be overcome by the great tiredness that suddenly descends upon a worker when he is nearing sixty — his eyes were growing dim, his hands became weak and dithery and his saliva, poisoned with alcohol and ether, began to come out as rank yellow spittle — then Boss received his notice. Two billion in fake money and a room in a dead barracks. Suddenly it occurred to him that he too was a worker. What a fright! What loneliness! Stripped bare and crushed in the wheels of a blind machine, Boss, a grain of sand, Boss, a splinter, all at once tumbled into the great sea of his class, right to its bed where there is neither light nor hope.

Above him rolled dark waves, 1919 and then 1921. Boss lay still and saw only revolutionary ships wrecked in battle coming to the bottom from time to time and settling down beside him. With flags on their broken masts and dead men on shattered decks. The best sons of mankind, its stormy petrels, the madly brave Rosa Luxemburg and Karl Liebknecht.

In those long hours of miserable idleness, Boss would take a box stuffed with now worthless money out from under the bed, and sit over it for evenings and sit over it for days.

The wallpaper in the room is grey with red specks faded with time — as if here and there had gushed a fountain of human life which spattered it and ran dry.

The veins in Boss's legs swelled up: his tired blood was begging to go back to the earth.

Tall and dressed in a coffee-coloured jacket, with a medal on his watch-chain and leaning on a crutch, he goes to meet his wife who, despite her grey hair, has started as a worker at the tobacco factory. Everyone in the area knows Minna — there are no other faces like hers. It is a whiter-than-white mark of such beauty that you want to stand up before it and bow to the ground. In his youth Boss was shrill, imperious and insistent, considering it his duty to torment her to keep the family's equilibrium. After work this face with tiny beads of sweat on the forehead shines like plaster-of-paris.

Through the walls of basements and attics, prisons and factories, there seeps and oozes the still, quiet river of labour solidarity, drops gathering into streams, streams into rivers and seas. With infinite patience it laps against stones and iron bars, undermining, gouging and washing away grain after grain of sand to break surface at the right day and hour in a torrent of indignation.

Such a day came for Boss, too. His neighbour, the cobbler, raised himself up to the first floor, took a rest, got himself to the second, knocked at the door and opened it. He had come to offer Boss an *Arbeiter Zeitung* (a communist newspaper).

A deep silence fell upon his lodging. The white Minna turned even whiter and hid in the kitchen. The cobbler sat down. The paper cost twenty pfennings. Boss, nearly choking in his tie, paid the twenty for it and flung on the table another, grey, spiked coin with a little ring on one side.

"Take that sh-t! That's all I've earned in my life."

The Iron Cross.

"Für Kriegshilfsdienst" (for war service behind the lines.) WR and a crown.

Slippers

These are warm comfortable slippers made of camel hair. Everyone thinks they are foreign, most often English, because of their checkered design and takes them in carriages on international trains. Four marks fifty pfennings a pair.

As a matter of fact these luxurious 'Anglo-Saxons' are made in the town of Hanau by special slipper seamstresses and at home what's more. The slippers are haughty, fearing to open their mouths and breathe lest they betray their lowly origin. They reek of poverty. Frau Kremer gets four marks for a hundred slippers. In an hour she can complete five. Her daughter, in only her second year in this job, can sew seven slippers in fifty-five minutes. To learn for forty years only to be beaten by the automatic advantage of energy. Like a cabman's horse. However many years it may have clattered its hooves on the road, its skill does not thereby increase. If she jabs the needle in at lightning speed, pressing it with her pet corn, it make no odds — she's already an old jade. Any country foal will outjump her simply because it is twenty years younger.

The maximum straining of effort cannot increase her earnings. The faster the needle flies, the more often the cheap, weak thread breaks and her employer gains also. It is all calculated and measured out so meanly that the seamstress not only cannot save a single pfenning but has to put in some herself.

It is very tempting to sew slippers padded with cotton-wool. A young working girl ignorant of the craft easily falls into that trap. For every warm pair the factory owner pays not ten but all of fifteen pfennings. But you won't catch Mrs. Kremer with such a bait. Let others burn their fingers: for she knows that it is all a matter of needles. Pushing through a double sole is harder than a normal one. But for both types you are supplied with exactly the quantity of needles. Three per hundred. As if she didn't know that with cotton-wool the most dexterous seamstress will break at least ten. And that's not all. The tricks and ruses by which the last drop of energy can be squeezed out of a human being are endless. It is easier to sail a ship around the Cape of Good Hope than to stitch a bulky sole so that not a single stitch can be seen.

Add it up: how many plain ones can a woman sew in an hour? Five. But with the padding, only three. An extra pfenning will go on needles but for the same sixty minutes the boss will give ten pfennings less. It is not for nothing that Frau Kremer with her hunched back, black rags and a wad of cotton-wool in her ear oozing with pus, resembles a statue of sorrow and distrust. If life itself passed right by her today with outstretched arms she would only purse her lips and hide her store of finished slippers further out of the way.

This room, with its sideboard without crockery, purple feather-beds which the fluff leaks out of, uncleared chamber-pot and a kitchen, with no water and no lavatory, whose ceiling, unpainted and unpatched for ten years, is peeling with soggy scabs and Frau Kremer herself, like a mouse fallen into an anthill and half-gnawed to pieces, all have but one means of defence: total distrust. They vote against everything. Frau Kremer says: the SPD are rogues, every word they say is a lie, and the communists are cowards. They let 1923 slip by. What does it matter to her whether the party was ready for struggle or how many more months or years of petty boring work might still be necessary in order to lead the proletariat to victory? And when will that be?!

She needs help now, at this minute, or otherwise never,

because Frau Kremer's energies are coming to an end and she is 'dying in harness'.

When a mouse is mortally terrified it starts to sweat. It becomes wet all over with fear. So where should Frau Kremer await the revolution, covered as she is with the perspiration of the final weariness?

"I cannot join a trade union. It is forbidden to work for such a low rate in the union. Then they'll demand that I give up the job."

But in Frau Kremer's home it's a big labour holiday: her one son, a fifteen-year-old boy employed at a cigar-box factory, is on strike for the first time in his life. The strike began three weeks ago and 135 people are taking part. Without a hope of success — strikebreakers are converging from neighbouring villages in droves.

The old woman is silent. Neither a word of reproach nor a single complaint. To be true to herself she acts as if nothing has happened, as if she does not notice his presence. After all, she doesn't believe in strikes, or socialism or even smallpox. Everything that originates from the masters is a big swindle. For a whole year she hid her grandson from the municipal doctor. Anyway they dragged him off to hospital the other day and pricked him all over and there, wasn't she right? Four pock-marks had opened up under the dirty shirt on his little arm.

But how Frau Kremer puts out her son's plate on the table and how she gazes at his tall manly back loafing around the larder! How she tells the neighbours, raising her eyebrows and guardedly expecting a rebuke:

"My son's on strike."

For being true to his class, for the solidarity that passes from generation to generation and the young courage that does not remember past defeats, the old dead tree waves its last branch to him without a sound.

He a Communist and She a Catholic

Workers who have been deprived of their livelihood because of their political unreliability belong mostly not to the younger but the older generation. The young peasant lad who is in the way in the house will go off to the factory whatever the wage and however long the hours if only to get himself a couple of marks for his beer, a bicycle and a fashionable suit with knee-breeches for Sundays. He eats and drinks at his father's for nothing. The older generation of workers that has passed through a twenty-five year school of trade union and revolutionary struggle is, in spite of its relatively high rates of pay and its position as an aristocracy of labour, far less compliant, having no desire to yield its final positions without a battle.

The result of any resistance, however cautious and moderate, is dismissal. At first the worker is not depressed. He has excellent references covering twenty or twenty-five years, a revival can be discerned in his trade and to-morrow if not today a vacancy will be created somewhere. Anyway his wife is working as a domestic help for the family of some well-to-do person and earns quite a decent wage.

At the beginning no one reminds him of the cruel law of unemployment. It comes into force by itself. The one who feeds the family becomes the head of the household. Returning from a hard day's stint he likes to sit down to a good spread laid on the table in a clean tidy dwelling. The children must be washed and brushed before his return, their noses wiped and their homework checked. But then, three days later, father slams the front door behind mother, meekly puts her apron on and sets about the housework. He does the dusting, cleans the windows with a cloth, washes the dishes, rinses out the rags he cleaned the pots and pans with, takes out the slops, sluices down the kitchen floor, makes the bed, hangs out the feather-bed over the window sill and when it has been warmed through in the sun puts it back in its place with meticulous care.

We Russians haven't the least conception of the ritual of cleanliness and order which the wife of an average or even the poorest German worker performs every day in her home. You can sit and watch her for hours, cleaning, washing and scrubbing her kitchen, crockery and linen. Not just flipping a wet rag round now and again like we do. No, under the divan, behind the stove, along the window-sill and in the farthest corners where no one ever peeps. All this must now be carried out by her reluctant husband. And just as in good times past he would run his finger along the stove to check that there was not a speck of dust and not forgive his wife for a single grain or a single spot missed, so now it is he who must answer to her. She is the head of the household who feeds the family. He is the subordinate, obedient domestic help, a nanny in trousers, a washer-up in his own hearth and home. In the depths of his soul every German regards his wife as his servant and looks down on her work. As he shuffles the wife's mop into the corners, sits over a bag of potatoes and gets the dinner ready the husband feels degraded beyond measure. These workers see things just as any petty-bourgeois does. One very good comrade who had been unemployed for several years said to me with deep bitterness, pointing to his sleeves rolled up to the elbows, with a brush in one hand and the wife's boot in the other:

"See what wretched humiliation unemployment brings us. I, a man, have to clean the old woman's shoes."

Insulted and injured in his masculine pride, a father attempts to restore the balance by other means. On pay day, when his wife will lay out her week's earnings on the table with a feigned modesty, he walks up and down all day, gloomy, irritable and pained. A furious scene erupts over dinner:

"Who's master in the house — you or me?"

The thump of a fist on the table. An old lash comes off the wall. The children scream. Mother begs forgiveness. After dinner the parents go off to the bedroom. He makes her beg for a long time. She gets undressed, staring at him with imploring eyes. He violates her with hatred and makes her cry out so loud that it can be heard on the staircase and finally sends her downstairs for some cigarettes. Never, even in the days of good money, had he loved his wife with such a jealous love; never had she fancied caresses more than now, when they had in effect to be bought.

A husband gradually turns into his wife's souteneur.

"I'll soon become her Alphonse," said little Kamm, the one

who was cleaning the boots. His situation is further complicated by the fact that his wife springs from an old-established catholic peasant family, with portraits of the Kaiser and Kaiser's wife, Augusta, masses on Sunday and a grandfather who is the standard-bearer of the veterans' association of the 166th Regiment of blue-and-yellow Uhlans. They had been against the marriage all along. Why on earth had he, a short, restless foundryman who changed bosses like gloves, married the tall, fine honest peasant maid! A little husband cannot keep a family! . . .

Now that Kamm has fallen into material dependence on the old folks, her family seeks to review the whole family constitution to the advantage of the wife and children and at the expense of the dissolute husband. Yes, little grandaughter Lieschen can spend the whole summer with grandpa and grandma and it won't cost a penny. On Saturdays they will send dumplings, lard and goose to the town but granddaughter must go to church and not miss a single mass. If the young ones want to be supported, father must tell the child that God exists and that all godless ones will land in hell. What can you do? You have to put up with it. Fortunately Lieschen shares her father's sceptical mind and his French guile. They understand each other by hints.

"Lieschen," says Kamm to his daughter, sitting her on his knees, "you remember I told you there isn't a God and that heaven is just a silly tale for children? Lieschen, look at me in the eyes: I made a mistake, I told you an untruth. He's really sitting up in the sky and he sees and knows absolutely everything."

The old folk are standing by him and watch their son-in-law's mouth like a card-player's hand. The little one nods:

"I see, daddy."

Kamm knows his own sort. "What a good thing the child is as cold as a dog's nose to all these tricks," he thinks.

Kamm has been out of work now for three years. He does the washing, bakes the bread and has learnt to darn stockings. There is no end to the reproaches. With continual talk about how the poor chap has driven his family to poverty, how the party makes use of men when they're working in the factory but abandon them in poverty, you can go out of your mind.

"What have you got for your privations? They haven't even appointed you as a minor official in the party!" He escapes from all this into work. In the winter he goes round the villages as a roving agitator; he ascends the Vögelsberg and climbs the Spessart hills. He is the first to have dared speak as a communist in public in a settlement of old Waldensians, erstwhile partisans of the great peasant wars and now rich peasants secludedly living a viciously miserly life far away from the world. Each of them is in fact wealthy, with up to sixty acres a piece but not a horse or a labourer to work them. Inflation has gobbled down their money but without machines and fertiliser how can you wring a crop out of the cold brutal ground? Deceived by the faith of their fathers and themselves, the village commune drove from the settlement both the priests and the recruiting agents of the various parties, the vote-hunters for the presidential elections. Kamm has not yet won a single supporter from among these embittered Old Believers, but it is only to him that the grim-looking old men in broad-brimmed medieval hats and their womenfolk in white caps looking like starched kites, give their greetings.

In the remotest upland settlements where it is almost impossible to till the soil because of the frequent rain that washes all the manure downhill, they know his face, which could pass for either eighteen or forty years of age, his satchel of newspapers and halting step.

"That chap's not satisfied with watching beans come up," the hewers from the basalt mines say of him, wild men, farm-hands, forest poachers, the dearest friends of the prince's deer that enjoy an immunity in the forests along the Rhine as if they were diplomats. It is quite true that Kamm does not have even a kitchen-garden or an allotment out of town with a summer-house and a lettuce-bed where the German proletarian potters about so happily after his day's work. The vicar of Griesheim whom they get tied up with on Sundays after the sermon once said of him:

"A spiteful, biting mouth" and "a poisonous little spider".

But all the mountain tracks lead down to the valley again.

After the long wanderings he has to go home. And at home there waits the pious, wicked wife, the tall beautiful peasant girl with the perpetually downcast eyes, imperious, greedy and burning. Twenty times Kamm has left never to return and twenty times he has turned back for Lieschen's sake — for "his own blood". If he goes off who will protect her from the priests, the old women and her mother's false beliefs?

The most horrible part, the retribution and punishment, begins when the children are already asleep, the door locked and the windows corked up; the whole *middle-class* house is obligingly silent and turns a blind eye.

Now she is undressing. An iron corset and savagely tightened, unpuncturable, fireproof breastplates. Alien in spirit, hostile to his every thought and booklet on his table, she is happy in his defeats and rejoices with his enemies yet she is more unscrupulous in bed than any street-girl. Would they ever! What prostitute could conjure up what the devout middle-class girl is up to on the quiet on a legal footing in her own home with the blinds down; with a husband obliged to love and satisfy her even though for her, he is, God forbid, not fit for anything else because of his idiotic communist ideas! He that does not work, neither shall he eat!

The sharper the encounter, the deeper the defeat that follows. Having taken her fill the woman sinks back like a swollen tick only to show at once, with her hair scarcely straightened and her nightdress still creased up, that "all that" can change nothing in their relationship. Everything remains as before.

"Don't forget to remind me, Hans, that tomorrow we have to buy a prayer-book for Lieschen, are you listening? The Old and the New Testaments."

In the Ruhr —
Under the Ground

"Sit down here and don't move! if anyone sees you and starts talking to you, keep your mouth shut!"

The door slammed and a miner's lamp tilted in the direction of the miners' shed. Shafts of light from the windows of the nearby generating plant lie like white leaves across the Works Committee's table. The walls are bare and a loud snore resounds from the shadows. Or so at least it seems. That's the compressor breathing, forcing air down underground. You count and measure those sighs with infinite jealousy. Is it better or worse than in Russia? The engineers pass by on their way underground for the night. Their shadows wave sleeves across the floor.

"Well, let's go. Take longer steps. Right hand in your pocket. And your cap further down."

Now the lift is hurtling into an abyss. A modest little cage. For the pit is not a large one. About eight hundred men are employed here — it has survived only because its coal can be tossed straight on to the Rhine. Yet this is the Ruhr, Germany's most technically developed region.

Two hundred, three hundred metres. Down the shaft's black gullet twinkle golden fissures marking the different levels. They clank with the sound of tub wheels and again the platform stands still while the damp slime of the walls, humming gloom and the depths rush to meet it at indescribable speed. Longer than a whole flight of stairs yet lasting only a few seconds during which the cage pulls up and settles carefully upon some levers which stretch upwards to meet it. It gropes blindly for the floor level although an underground station with bright lighting, trains and people stands right in front of it.

The air which had been stuffed into your ears like cotton-wool has now leaked out.

From the black galleries somebody seems to be calling out in Russian, so intelligible are the sounds of the pair of rails disappearing into the darkness, converging towards the sloppy churned-up mud between them, the pony's neighing, the smell of dung from a stable nearby and the quiet singing of water braiding its streams into plaits over the coals. No matter where he comes from the foreigner will read the signs of international labour on these German walls with a private shiver and a sure and deep excitement. For the stillness of the pit is filled with a wordless tongue common to all the world. The earth's alphabet is even simpler than tapping on prison cell walls. Its runic characters are made of tough pine and the branches and crowns of oak. You find yourself smiling! What thin trunks are used here for the pit's backbone, what slender graceful trees. They stand as if on a forest fringe in the calm before a storm, bent to one side. On them lies the weight of mountains. They heed the course of these ranges and are bent by their imperceptible motion. The cavity behind the bulkheads has to firmly be stopped up with boulders. The overman walks up and down these coops woven out of the wood. The stones peep between the twigs and touch his hands with their dumb muzzles and cold animal snouts. Isn't there more space out there? Has that demonic gravity, crushing down to entomb, squeezed in from behind? Can he really not throw open this grave, stick his feet into the earth's belly and push it back with his untiring hands?

Beware! On the wet wall the pit writes one warning after another with its wooden joists, just as a deaf-mute forms letters from matchsticks. Can't you see how badly the work has been done here? Stonefalls give a hollow ring. Cold leaks out of the cracks. Here there is nothing, there is a void and over there it will fall out, pour through and slide down. And pressing, pressing down unbearably.

At a glance all is in order. The neat and carefully made pit almost resembles an underground farm. There are no luxuries or signs of special opulence but everything is in place and fits well. The concrete areas are bright as gold and fresh straw gleams in the stables. The plump well-fed ponies can each pull fifteen loaded tubs and push up to four in front with their chests. The water brought here from the other levels murmurs peacefully as in a village mill. At the end of the western gallery a dam stands like a bastion. Behind it a well has been sealed off: a few years ago a drunk drank himself silly and drowned himself. They had tried to push forward in that direction but snakes of water shot out with such an evil hiss and an unexpectedly high pressure that the breach had to be plugged quickly with a concrete cork. Since then there has been order and calm in that sector too; the pony-men, like shepherds, have simply stopped driving their flocks that way.

But alarm signals persist from the steps along the very first offshoots branching off the main trunk. Why hasn't the timbering been replaced for so long? Nearer the light stand dry trunks treated with a special compound that protects them from damp. Oak is like iron. But this costly method has evidently been dropped years ago. Dampness happily flowers in frothy sponges everywhere. Whole rows of clean trees suffer from it like a bad disease. They stand in silence not letting each other down. Only the water quietly sniggers as the overman unpicks their porous skin with his lantern hook to reveal immediately soft wet reddening flesh.

Keep walking. You are soon in a dark side-burrow. My legs, spread apart, fumble along the upper joist; the roof pressing on my head comes down lower. Here are the old corridors where coal is no longer won. They look like drunkards, wandering now to one side and now the other, getting booted back by the mass pressing on either side. Barely managing to make the exit, they drop their rotting crutches and feel the ceiling settle down on to their necks. Broken, snapped, crushed props are everywhere. As if after a pogrom. A naked imprint of neglect, miserliness and poverty lies upon it. You stumble at every step on traces of a criminal thrift and a wretched fear of expenditure.

The footsteps that passed slowly by us behind the wall belonged to the boss's son-in-law, a former Prussian officer. During the coal crisis economising extended even to the staffing of the pit. In 1918 this young man knew nothing about mining. Although he did not manage to complete his course and gain a qualification he can now in these hard times replace a dismissed overman. Ever since economising on wood, nails and even lamp-oil started anxiety has increasingly often driven this man with his old soldier's sense of duty underground. He shouts at the workers, telling them off for extravagance and for not knowing how to save on materials. That is why as soon as the men turn away he rushes to the face, studies the joists, squeezes himself into its every corner, taps and eavesdrops on the danger with a quaking heart. This individual surprises the workers day and night with his unexpected appearances and it's hard to say what they hate him most bitterly for: the affected coolness with which he drives them to work in dangerous, poorly reinforced places, those miserable pangs of conscience and fear of responsibility oozing from every pore of his pale, puffy face, or that infinite lack of self-confidence that saps the courage of others. A boorish animal that cares nothing for itself and cuts short other men's fear would be better than this miserable sergeant-major in whom an antiquated sense of honour rots and stinks like a bad tooth.

In that night of subterranean roving we nevertheless ran into him at one of the crossroads. He was sitting on the ground propped up against the wall, his lamp between his sharp knees. Two workers were silently clearing stones that had collapsed on the railway track to the accompaniment of his monotonous, persistent droning. Sweat shone on their bare backs trickling down their ribs to wash out white gashes in their black skins. Meanwhile the manager went on sitting and scourging them with the birch rod of his tedious discourse. The muscles of the men at work swelled and crawled in front of him in silence.

"Let me tell you: had you not stabbed us in the back in 1918 everything would have been different. Yes, the seven-hour day too and we wouldn't have had to save on every pfenning. Look, for instance, this ceiling could cave in and kill one of you. Who would be to blame? In your opinion, the boss. No, not the boss. Yourselves. You should not have had the revolution."

The overman fell silent all of a sudden and his ears pricked up like an animal's. What did he take fright at? True, there is a boiler nearby where rising air deposits its moisture. Every tap, every blow resounding in the most remote part of the pit echoes through its depths with a quiet rustle. The boiler lies still, listens, and rings like a seashell in the stillness.

What was it? Or did I imagine it? Of course I did. The cast-iron vessel again hisses as if rocking a baby crying in its sleep. A nauseating fear. You can see someone else spew up and you feel queer yourself. One of the workers lifts his eyes, filled with deep hatred, towards the overman but he had moved off in time.

The pit is a black book. Telling how the earth makes war on man and also how, here under the ground, man, the boss, makes war on his own workers. Water washes away walls, erodes ceilings and rots wooden structures. While behind the miners' backs walks the owner, forcing them to work rapidly and carelessly, plundering the wood of the timbers for his own use, dragging out every superfluous prop from the face, tugging every bit of wood from the creeping walls and snatching every spare joist from menacingly overhanging ceilings. He looses danger from its chain and unties death's hands to gain the extra penny. He is a marauder looting his own army and sending it into battle with rotten weapons into positions that he himself has undermined, weakened and surrendered.

The Works Committee does everything possible to obstruct such 'business activity' by the pit-owner. My escort, I won't mention his name or his face — let the brim of his miner's cap conveniently cover his coal-smeared features — swings his lamp to the right and left to dispel the importunate blackness weighing in on all sides, and from time to time slaps the wall with his hand and strokes the coal like a black horse with a dewy-wet mane. He says with pride: "This is our doing. See those iron brackets that secure the steep ladders? Before, they stood free. A miner'd risk his life using them. See the oblong manhole in the floor covered by the wooden hatch? Management bargained about it till one of the workers whose lamp had gone out fell through and was killed. See those steel bolts: the two bars jutting up where the railway track suddenly breaks off at the edge of the shaft? They cost the lives of several of us and were got at the cost of a strike. They weren't there before. A pony would trot gaily forward with its tub, put its coal on the platform and then go back. Sometimes the lift would be late and then the tub, pony and driver would drop into the void. Over there in the wall is a new strut. Several nails stick out of it. I have the authority to rip those clean out and fine the overman for negligence because in the event of the smallest landslide this thing with nails on the end could kill a man. Only two or three years ago I couldn't have done so."

Throughout the colliery there is evidence scattered of the Works Committee's small victories but down the deep shafts lie its defeats in graves. Drifting up from those cellars sealed up by reaction comes a hollow groaning. Down below, those buried alive raise their fists to the roofs of their earthen coffins in impotent rage. There all is crushed, disillusioned, filled with distrust and despair.

The coal face. From far off the miners' movements seem somehow strange. Or do they just appear so through the dim lamp-light? If lunatics can go on with their work without opening their eyes, their arms constrained by deep slumber, they would undoubtedly move like those face-workers repairing the coal-shute. The oldest of the three workmates sits a little on one side on a pile of new boards and watches our approach with completely white eyes. He is fast asleep and his eyelids, unsoiled by coal-dust, stand out in the middle of his face like two cataracts. He can now hear his name mentioned and the light from our lamps strikes those pale shades; yet he still cannot open them. Eventually they lift slowly like an iron curtain.

"Why are you still here?"

"We're not leaving tonight."

"Your shift finished a long while ago."

"We're now on the third shift here. He didn't let us off."

Previously the boss had permitted these three workmates, who lived some fifty kilometres from D. and came to work by rail, to leave the face ten minutes before time. Not out of the kindness of his heart but because the gang is virtually the best in the mine and to lose such men just for the sake of a few minutes was not worthwhile. Today the foreman met them by the lift and sent them back. Their train left without them of course. To go home by the next one in the middle of the night would mean being late for the morning shift. Lateness means dismissal. Having waited at the station for two hours they went back below ground. So they crept back here not knowing what to do, humiliated, tired, perhaps already unemployed. The coal sparkles under their hacks like the snow of this hard winter they are all thinking about, lifting their heads longingly towards a narrow crack as if morning would dawn through the thickness of the earth.

Two were not in any party and one was an old convinced SPD man. When he realised what was afoot, the Menshevik worker quickly put his implement down and lowered himself so as to stand guard at the nearest corner.

"But relieve me when you lot have had your say. I want to hear about Russia too."

Three times night had swung the heavy gong of its clock and above the bell had rung three times, but the pit in its dark depths could not hear this ring. Dangling their legs over the edge of their hole and bringing their lamps closer in, the face-workers, the night-lights of their coal-ringed eyes gleaming, read out but were unable to conclude an indictment that was at the same time a long night's story-telling. They took it in turns, passing the tale from one to another in the same way as one tired worker passes his pick to the next. None of them could remember the experience of the revolution as a whole. For them it was a history that stretched back over a whole decade, one of strikes badly fought and lost. A man does not die from all the wounds he receives. Each of the miners had lost faith in socialism from one specific betrayal or one single act of treachery. Here, the old man had been poisoned by the toxic gases of *Vorwärts's* articles against Russia; there the fragments of a smashed strike had crippled the young worker. A speech by Noske had burst like shrapnel over the third. There are also very recent injuries, no more than a few days or weeks old.

For example the SPD worker who was standing on guard had been lost recently, in 1924, when the unions broke the last big strike of Ruhr mineworkers only three days prior to the verdict of the conciliation commission, despite the feeling of the masses and notwithstanding the fact that the strike had lasted twenty-five days and could have held out as long again. They smashed the moment's solidarity, preventing the transport workers' union from coming to the aid of the coalminers; in this way they helped the metalworkers betray their comrades so that to this day the treachery has not been forgotten among workers.

They whipped up discord, sowing a caste hostility between the different branches of labour, salting and teasing this wound on the body of the proletariat. Comrade T., forgetting all caution, no longer spoke but shouted at the top of his voice. His coal-matted beard stuck out from his face like a stake.

"The Saar goes on strike but we work. Didn't you see? Hundreds of trains ready at all the stations? They started to move as soon as the strike in England began. They even called it 'English coal."

"I'm an old social democrat and these two here are honest working men but together we were strikebreakers. And our party urges workers to do the work of traitors. Oh yes, the unions talk to us like the Kaiser used to: *'Kumpels, raus oder du kriegst eine.'* (Get out, mate, or you'll get one.) Where's all this going to end? What will they do with a hundred thousand unemployed?" The old man laughs, the face around his eyes has grown dim like a piece of rain-drenched canvas. "Well, they'll put us in a compound and set the machine-guns up around. *Sie haben noch Mätzger genug! Darum kriegen wir Schlag wie junge Hunde."* (they've got enough butchers so we'll be beaten up like puppies.)

Communists had been to see the old man and had offered him in vain their own world-view, unstained by betrayal of the proletariat. After the great disappointment that social democracy has brought them people are so distrustful and fearful that they will no longer take anything from others. Let's see if communism hits the capitalist like a good rifle. They break it up into pieces (to see if there are any tricks in it) and string together out of the assorted damaged pieces a naive home-made weapon, the trade union. The defeats of the last years have shown: struggle is impossible without them. So the *Kumpels,* digging themselves into their dark lairs, had dreamt up a utopia. It was built up around Lenin's name and the fragments of his teaching which had already penetrated down here underground. Lenin had said that the cell must be at the point of production. In one way or another he had expounded this idea many times. Why is it that the party goes after workers in the factories and mines and is not afraid of their dirty flats, while the unions sit somewhere up on high beyond reach and just give orders? They ought to come down here underground to the face so that it'd be just as easy to grab the union by the scruff of the neck as to reach up for your bottle on the wall for a drink.

"Kein Berlin, keine grossen Menschen. Hier, hier, mit uns!" (No Berlin, no big shots. Here, with us here!) Not knowing how better to express his idea, comrade T. lifted his lamp up to some new props driven into the wall. There in the twilight some blind grey subterranean butterflies were swarming round the pine-log. Wherever you have timber you have this semi-translucent moth as well; eating the moisture and sipping the darkness together, dwelling together and rotting together. "That's how our unions ought to be!"

"Goodbye, comrades! Maybe we'll meet again in different circumstances."

"No. We pretty certainly won't live that long."

I can't remember at which end or whether it was deeper or higher in that underground labyrinth: possibly it was on a pony-man's plank-bed in a hidden corner where the overman doesn't peep very often and you can stretch out for half an hour, blissfully resting your legs and sense just the draughts and a peculiar chill seeping up like the earth's breath through the cracks into the hard bed, through your clothes to the body — possibly it was on just such a plank-bed that there was a burly old man, a Bavarian peasant. Standing behind in rows like stooks in a field are the years he has worked. He has not counted them and has not looked back. He has not known politics but cut coal clinging to the ground with his peasant's clamp-like feet. He has twice been to war but even then did not wake up — a worker without thoughts, all his life a farmhand. Only the recent Reichstag law on invalids forced him even to raise his head. Under this law sixty-year-old miners will receive nothing from the state. They will have to go back to the pit for a further five years to await the alms-giving. Old G. had walked towards his pension over mountains of coal like an ox going home from the field dreaming of rest and a night's sleep. But suddenly right at the gate where he could scent habitation, hear the dogs barking and see lighted windows, he had to turn round and go back into the night, the cold, deep earth. G's huge hands, rakes with which he has raked up so much coal during his life, lie heavy on his knees and he stares at them: they are too heavy. He'd like to take them off and lay them down on the coal by his shovel and pick.

"After work I'll have to have a glass of vodka in the tavern." Then suddenly pain wells up through his whole body: there's no money for that glass. But how had it been reckoned? He's worked for sixty years but hasn't got himself enough for some *Schnapps*. *"Schuften und schuften auf meine alte Tag."* (Slaving and slaving until my old age.) His grandfather and great-grandfather had been peasants. He is a ploughman too and has ploughed his whole life: he has turned over and dug the earth and thrown into the mine's black furrows the seed of his strong peasant years. He has sown and sown and nothing has grown. Not a single grain has come up. Not one has borne a crop. Deep down in that ravine there lingered a confused thought about the absurdity and ugliness of life and an irony that bursts through the clods of his benumbed brain like a brook from under a stone.

'Wait till I pass away, then I'll stick my hands in my pockets!"

Only after having wandered like this under the ground, warming yourself first at one lamp and then another shining like a watch-fire in the middle of the coal-face, peering into dozens of faces emerging one after another from the gloom and listening to those voices coming out of the dark keyholes of the earth do you begin to realise *what* today, in these years of defeat, connects the German worker with Russia. There was no crevice, no lair at the bottom of which they would not be talking about the Land of the Soviets, like exiles abroad talk of a distant homeland.

Even the gloomiest, the most backward and the most defeated men on whom the whole burden of stabilisation lies. Linked to the idea of Russia is another hope which they cherish and nurture in the pits' deep darkness and thousands, each in his own way, think about and jealously guard from the corrupting contact of the victors. At present it is but a pale, weak shoot growing up without sunlight, by the light of a wretched miner's lamp. The idea of working-class unity.

On the first face: "Man alone made war — so why is unity impossible in the world?" "Let our delegation come back. What it says will settle everything. *Nach dem wird sich alles richten.*" (After that everything will be all right.)

On another: *"Wenn die Verbänd nicht in einem Topfgekocht werden — sind wir kaput."* (If the unions don't all get in together, we've had it.)

"Why are the capitalists united and not us?"

"Why did the railwaymen laugh when we were on strike?"

"Mensch, man hat a Spass daran, wenn die Hand gehen." (It'll be pretty good, pal, when we march together.)

On a third, the deepest and blackest: "Please convey our thanks to the Russian workers for the grain sent in the 1924 strike, for it reached us in time of need. Everything else has been stolen by our unions; they gobbled from the strike fund with big spoonfuls."

Ullstein

No one runs to fetch the news from the telegraph office: it arrives on its own. Wild swallows beat against the floor right in front of the editor's desk and lie down before him already complete and translated into the human tongue and printed out by a little gadget on to a narrow ribbon of paper. Ten small machines receive and tap out continuously. A dark monastery with a hundred cells. A hundred telephone booths. A hermit in each invoking the god of sensation with a wild cry:

"This is Berlin, *B.Z.* [*Berliner Zeitung*] This is Ullstein. Hallo! Speak up!"

Messengers are dozing like the unemployed on park benches. Like passengers waiting for trains that are always arriving, every minute departing but never standing still. A train of news girdling the globe. Many have been waiting since the previous evening. They have already met the specials from America and the Entente Express packed with flighty little stock-exchange bulletins, those bewitching adventuresses that slip unnoticed over the border with a skimpy luggage of fake news, that priceless contraband so hunted by newspapermen.

Well, Ullstein's home is large enough to accommodate all comers. 4,500 rooms, six floors, staircases like elevator chutes, a dozen separate print-shops — the best mills in Germany grinding a daily harvest of lies and truth — and six newspapers that bake the daily bread for Berlin's millions, all its layers of population, both sexes and all ages, for Germany as a whole and for each of her cities individually. Cologne does not eat what Berlin likes; Dresden's favourite dish will not find a customer in Frankfurt. For the Hamburg docker, *Knackwurst* with porter, for Dresden, *Eisbein* and cabbage while for the southerners anything that is light, nourishing and dainty.

Nobody travels on foot in Ullstein's house. Idlers can climb the stairs. Here people fly by lift. Running past all the floors are its open cages. The door has been done away with and the liftman gone the way of the ichthyosaurus. This lift stops nowhere and waits for no one. People leap on to one of its platforms while moving and leap off it while moving. Proofs, copy and telegrams follow a course in practical gymnastics. Leading articles, weighty feuilletons and paunchy, corpulent, short-breathed political commentaries have all become acrobats and circus artistes. They run from building to building, crossing the yard on a wire, flying up and down at a hair-raising speed hardly catching hold of the electric postman's wire basket. From the day that Ullstein senior built his first shed on the Kochstrasse — a small print-shop — his business has grown ceaselessly. Once it reaches a certain level of perfection it stops and gobbles up its old body. The day that the ever self-renewing spirit of industry dare not and cannot club its own skull or digest in its own stomach obsolete modes of organisation, technique and business management it will become breakfast for a more flexible and powerful competitor. Take the old *Berliner Morgenpost:* it had grown up out of a cemetery — not of its obsolete methods but of the entire social-democratic press destroyed by Bismarck. It was then that Ullstein proved able to throw hundreds of thousands of copies of his moderate street news-sheet on to a deserted newspaper market — into the breach made by the Anti-Socialist Law. It was a paper aimed at the broadest mass of the petty bourgeoisie.

How often have methods of work changed since then! From hand setting to mechanical setting, from drawings to photography and then from anaemic smudgy colourless photos to artistic montage. After each technical revolution, a brief incapacity for the whole concern as after a vaccination. Then a frantic leap forward — the prey: hundreds of thousands of new subscribers, new buildings, workshops, staff, drivers, lorries and telephones. Over the recent post-war years appendicitis has again set in in the newspaper plant's body: now it is the old type-casting machines, English machines that run on gas and have to be always full of molten tin otherwise they don't work. German machines have been brought in to replace them: they devour plain and simple coal and can be topped up when you wish — from one cardboard mould you can get thirty metal castings.

The works knows no gratitude nor remembers past services rendered. Life has left the old section. It is cold and empty and a lazy fire lit in the furnace of its rivals is reflected in its dead window-panes. The merry clank of matrixes and files brushing their hot edges drift up to the now banished section like the clatter of knives on plates.

At one time only one newspaper was produced and they were afraid to put out an evening one lest its circulation be reduced. Today Ullstein, like a clever madame, sends dozens of papers into the street, distinctly dressed, speaking different tongues, landing on the pavement at different times and not getting in each other's way. Like prostitutes, they share the street between them and do not quarrel. Each one has its customers,. In the morning, *Vossische Zeitung,* intended for the stock exchange and the banks. She latches on to the smart operators as they stand in Aschinger's with sandwich in cheek and mug of beer in hand. She gets into the car with them and has time to do her business with them in the five minutes between restaurant and stock exchange or station and office. A clever, prudent and very well-informed newspaper, edited by one of the best German journalists. Every speculator hopes his fifteen pfennings will elicit something useful from it.

While the husbands are in town, Ullstein's *Die Praktische Berlinerin, Die Dame* or *Blatt der Hausfrau* call at their wives' doors. The last-mentioned is a masterpiece of technique. For this commercial traveller to run from house to house, inflaming appetites with whispers about the cheapest coffee-pot, a house-coat at 3.70 marks, a double-bed and a pregnancy remedy, typographical technique has accomplished a real miracle and human genius has arisen to a new level. In one shot the machine not only prints 96 pages of text and cover but also cuts, collates and folds them ejecting the completely finished issue into a tray. In this way 3,500 copies can be produced in an hour. What can be said about the needlework section and the patterns for cheap night-caps which *Die Dame* supplies its subscribers free of charge? Before anything has time to take shape in the mind of the woman instinctively putting money by for a future purchase as a bird gathers straw for a nest, her day-dreams have been already anticipated and snipped out in cigarette paper by Ullstein's cutters. The spirits of overcoats to be, spirits of blouses and trousers to be, nod towards the customer from out of the fog of the future and the tinsel never-never land of fresh clichés.

There are horses that can solve problems and dogs that know geography but what inconceivable intelligence a machine may acquire no one yet knows. Hoffmann's mechanical Olympia sang romantic songs and took her curtsey — but that's nothing. At Ullstein's a worker sits in front of a machine and types on a keyboard. He has pressed a letter. It immediately breaks out of its place and lies down at the beginning of the line. That is the first cross of the game. Next to it a second, a third and then in two seconds the whole line is moulded from the tin and leaps on to the galley. What do the letters do once the word they have formed is no longer needed? They demobilise. They go off to their homes. The machine lowers its long black arm, snatches up the used composition and places it on a special track along which each letter runs until it tumbles like a key into a keyhole.

Old Ullstein's youngest daughter comes on the streets at noon. She is a newspaper like a lizard or a fly: the fastest, most persistent and accessible of the sisters. Anyone can catch her on the wing and for next to nothing. She has neither her own opinion nor her own voice; she is a little puddle in which the whole world is reflected. In two minutes in a language intelligible to anyone she can re-state in the simplest crudest form what the big press is saying and thinking that day. Don't chew this news over: it has been well chewed up already, moistened with saliva and fully cooked by the *B.Z.* One swallowing action and you are informed. The man who has no time to think or collect his own information cannot live without this final, lowest and handiest intermediary, this echo of big cities, this flying street gramophone. She is born from the waste pipes of all the newspapers and lives for half an hour. Her appearance is eagerly awaited. Millions of people look at their watches as they await their rendezvous with *B.Z.* Yet no one is so quickly forgotten and no one is abandoned with such disdain on bus seats, cafe tables, the floor or underfoot. Every day there emerges from the froth of the streets this queen of the left-overs, a little tigress with a million customers.

12.10 p.m. The first bulletin is posted at the stock exchange. 12.12 p.m. The last telegram is received in the composing room. 12.15 p.m. The editors stop accepting copy. 12.16 p.m. The rotary press puts on its armour of gleaming plates. 12.17 p.m. The duty engineer switches the current on. The continent's largest rotary presses are beginning their morning's work.

The pages flow like water on a mill-wheel. A word is no more than a microbe in their torrent. The first finished, collated copies edge into view. And off they trip into the world with the staccato bark of machine guns. This is the morning assault, the crossfire of the press, shooting that neither misses nor misfires. Every sheet will be read by someone. Every cartridge will fall on somebody. The boom of the offensive hangs over the walls. They steam like waterfalls or like the brink of a mountain in eruption. The paper slowly revolves in the fire of this speed like a white whale on a spit. Rolls of it cover all the floor, gigantic cocoons of lies from which millions of ephemeral butterflies will flutter.

The factory is like a fortress. Its deep yards, separated from the city by mountains of granite, resemble those of a prison. In the event of siege a fortress must have a stock of water and bread. Ullstein has an energy source independent of the city that can feed his besieged machines for a week. A strike or an uprising. Armour-plated doors will close and within three minutes of the alarm signal generators will be sending thousands of horse-power of electric strikebreakers to the machines. None of the employees will go in or out of the gates unnoticed. The doorkeepers have been drilled on people and objects. But at 12.18, that is eight minutes after receiving the last urgent telegram, all the sluices are raised and all the doors opened wide. The newspaper plant overflows into the street. Conveyor tubes vomit bundles straight on to lorries. Light motor-bikes stand throbbing, waiting their turn. Cyclists hold open their bags. The couriers who travel with the newspapers to the station or to the provinces drop their unfinished lunches. On a Saturday 400 tons are loaded in all. Twenty mail trains taking a single lunch-time paper. Counting the other publications that means 75 mail coaches in three-quarters of an hour.

A newspaper outstrips time. A newspaper overtakes the hands of the clock. A human being sleeps for half his life. He steals the night hours for himself. Clearing the hurdle of speed, the news-paper stumbles over an insuperable obstacle: it cannot surmount a barricade of snoring night-caps. But in the cities and on the asphalt that gleams like ice everything is relative. Dawn can put on pyjamas instead of its out-moded morning clouds; from now on Europe will be like Greenland or the Arctic Ocean. Its electric day is continuous. At half past eight in the evening the news vendors come to do their morning turn outside Aschingers (and Aschingers are everywhere). The provincial edition of the *Vossische Zeitung,* without the final telegrams that are printed and transmitted at night, goes on sale in Berlin at 8.40 in the evening. A piece of tomorrow, a piece of the future, with football results, the names of the dreamers who have fallen under motor cars and English House of Commons debates can be bought for fifteen pfennings.

Ullstein is one of the great powers levying a duty on any vulgarity that can be imported into man's consciousness. His place is like a wharf where they discharge ocean-going ships of phrases that fit on to the consciousness like rubber protectors on down-at-heel boots, unloading witticisms that are as flat as the soles, smutty anecdotes and political slogans. The masterpiece in this genre, one without par, is of course the *Berliner Illustrierte Zeitung,* the most widely distributed magazine in modern Germany. 1,600,000 readers. And still growing. In six months it will probably reach two million. The foundation upon which Ullstein stands today is a propaganda machine of vulgarity. In reality it is a cipher, a nothing, a zero. Thirty-two pages of laxative ease. A peephole drilled into the boudoir of a celebrated film star, a chink through which anyone can spy on beautiful women in the bath from Spitzbergen to the Cape of Good Hope. A fragment of a novel so racy and banal that you can read it in the lavatory. Adverts. A prince's wedding. Another advert. Ten pages of adverts.

The *Illustrierte* has never been an enemy of Soviet Russia. German workers may have learnt more from it about the real, true face of the USSR than from anywhere else. It provides everything interesting and unexpected. Russia is a sensation. The *Illustrierte* provides Russia. Her streets, demonstrations, crowds, leaders, avenues, army and children's homes.

The practical, sober-minded businessman more readily believes in an established stable government than in one still existing only in the heads of Kurfurstendamm and Tauentzienstrasse residents. If the Bolsheviks can hold out another five years Ullstein will treat the White emigres just as his previous government treated Russian students after 1905: anyone subverting the legal power, even if Soviet, will be a revolutionary, a bomb-thrower and a crook. Yet while Ullstein insures himself for all risks and is generally friendly towards the USSR he quietly prints the White Guard *Rul* in one of the secluded corners of his home.

Friendliness is all very well but when the entire press raises a hue and cry against Bolsheviks Ullstein cannot remain silent. After printing news items that are amicable towards us in Russia for a whole year, he suddenly pounds away with all his heavy guns and, when repeated 1,600,000 times, his words echo more loudly than Moses' Commandments from the ancient mountain of the Hebrews. 'A New Crime of Bolshevik Justice' 'Three German Scholars Sentenced to Death'. Not just 'three scholars' but three times 1,600,000 'Kindermanns' and three times 1,600,000 'Bolshevik murderers'. And here it is not a zero any more but a social motor of a power and capacity of which there are few in Europe.

The *Illustrierte* does not give its brief, acid, political formulas in statistical columns and curves — no, it tattooes them on a music-hall artist's velvet skin, a celebrated ballerina's underwear or a bottle of scented water for removing foul odours from the armpits. This is where the indelible words 'War on Bolshevism', 'War on World Revolution' and 'War on Murderers of Innocent Shortsighted White-haired Kindermann with his Travelling First-Aid Kit' are in fact branded, stitched and written. Whatever the slogan Ullstein might launch — for or against Russia, for or against the Chinese Revolution, for the pact or against the pact — footballs fly into the sky with these slogans. *B.Z.'s* motor boats and yachts furrow the seas, its racehorses leap barbed-wire fences, *B.Z.'s* favourite cracks a top American boxer's nose and *B.Z.'s* motor-cycle sets a new speed record — in preference to any political watchword. A dog show, tennis, swimming, a prize for the best pedigree bull. Europe follows such things with the closest attention. Every proper newspaper has a page of sport each day. Its champions are far better known than the most important political figures. Ullstein was about the first to discover this gold-mine. He established a special department while others still had the fire reporter covering the races and matches. He took on a special editor, despatched plenipotentiaries to all Europe's totalisators and attached special correspondents to all the famous stables.

Ullstein understands nothing about art. For such subtleties and for the editorial board of *Querschnitt,* an aesthetic magazine printed on vellum paper for a few hundred subscribers, he has hired himself a gentleman, a connoisseur of old porcelain and all the eighteenth century snuff-boxes the world has seen. This magazine is a lily that seems to be wholly unconnected with the midden from which such vulgar grasses as *B.Z.* and the *Illustrierte* grow. It floats on the surface of Ullstein's millions, fragrantly smelling of negro sculpture and the shine of old Friedrich's jackboots in Menzel's pictures. It presents very artistic and very naked drawings intended for the connoisseur. When old Ullstein sees all this refinement, he snorts and curses. But the other editors, manufacturers of that terrible pulp literature, are forbidden to interfere in the aesthetes' affairs. Leave the Apollos to root around on their own for although they might not bring in any income they do attract people of circumstance and taste into the building. It's always good to keep a classical Venus in the entrance hall.

But for the manufacture of such goods as *Die heitere Friedolin,* old Ullstein has no need for assistants. Here he is the craftsman and specialist. Nobody knows better than he how much suet, margarine and sugar should be sprinkled into those little ten-pfenning booklets with a cycling dog on the cover, specifically designed to pollute, poison and degrade children's fantasies. They go out in 35,000 copies; 700,000 a month. A mixture of Pinkerton, circus, and a newsreel of crimes and slush. Its hero is a police dog with the soul of a *Vossische Zeitung* Sunday supplement reader.

Now about those romances: before the war a little 250-page book with a wedding or a noble suicide would cost about a mark. Today two. Never will any 'immortal' be read as these hacks are. Who is Tolstoy and who is Goethe by comparison with the Mr. Weber who wrote *Yes, Yes, Love?* Good old Ullstein deals with literature as a camel does a date. He makes his reader pull back and chew it over again. Immediately upon publication all Ullstein's romances are filmed in Germany's studios. The shop-girl, school-mistress and post-clerk require a faith in good fortune. The petty-bourgeois must learn that an honest man can achieve anything — a villa, a motor car, his own shop — without bloodshed, without violence and without struggle. Reading it is not enough. You have to see it. So Ullstein shows it. Anyone can go along and be convinced about how honest Alice with her neatness, good figurework and rather pretty little mug, could find her way into the world of the financiers. Stinnes marries her. Except that this Stinnes is as young and handsome as an assistant in the outfitting department at Wertheim's. Old people who have worked for a hundred years die rich. Look at their funeral corteges. Isn't it worth being obedient your whole life if it means that you can drive to 'rest' with those pompons and white top-hats? Not to mention the workers and petty clerks who all regularly win 200,000 and marry the boss's daughter.

Why have a revolution? What's the point of politics? Millions of European workers live with a dream about Russia. Millions of SPD workers privately cling to a hope for it . . . Workers send their delegations to Russia. But Ullstein's reader, the petty-bourgeois, goes to the pictures to see his promised land.

Ullstein is not alone of course. Competing with, and possibly outgrowing him, are newspaper publishers like the former Scherl Verlag that created in Germany a sort of 'non-party' paper now in the hands of Hugenberg, a former Krupp manager. Having seized what had belonged to a king of newspapers, Hugenberg converted these old 'non-party' papers, to which the average German philistine had grown accustomed, into mouthpieces of the most vehement and rabid counter-revolution. Following them are Mosse and many others who are more and more monopolising the newspaper and book market. There are many Ullsteins . . .

The tribute that these factories of bourgeois ideology rendered the government during the war cannot be overestimated! There were no pores in the social organism and no cells in its brain which they could not penetrate and for which a special toxin was not developed. Ullstein, Mosse and Hugenberg drove more than a few nails into the great wooden Hindenburg that then stood beside parliament opposite the Victory Column. Under the cocaine of their literature armies of men allowed themselves to be slaughtered. And without the aid of the newspaper trusts the government could never have pumped out of the petty bourgeois mass all the millions it extorted for the war loan.

Junkers

Like any true scientist, Professor Junkers had to break out of the university and leave its walls for ever in order to devote himself to science. This he did in 1909 along with his colleague and assistant, Doctor Mader, whose slighty askance, motionless gaze was fixed upon internal combustion engines as much then as today, nearly twenty years later.

Yet neither scientist had left the gymnasium at Aachen to take up aviation. The flying machine interested them no more than any other machine. But the university demanded that they teach certain subjects to ignorant little boys. So they gave up the university and pursued their experiments in peace and quiet.

If flying had ever been an art rather than a craft it was surely in those years. It engaged dreamers, sportsmen, adventurers and martyrs. They fashioned funny little boxes out of sail-cloth, a few brittle wires and matchboard and upon these paper kites flew or fell wholly at the will of fate — from the standpoint of 1925, a year of calm reckoning — irrationally, brilliantly and in profound ignorance. Nearly every contest ended in disaster. Two or three times a day spectators would jump over the fence and run across to the spot where a heap of fragments lay smouldering in the middle of the field. As many front-line aviators perished in a few days as in a whole year today. Mankind cleared its path to the sky on paper wings spattered with blood.

Professor Junkers had nothing in common with that noble lunacy. After many years' toil in the quiet of his office he just took one of technology's commanding heights and as a result of the conquest a most interesting and unresearched area fell to him. When the prisoners were being counted, there appeared that capricious aviation that had never before surrendered to anyone's hands. So Professor Junkers decided to give it a thoroughly scientific upbringing.

One of the basic ideas of this scientist who produced a revolution in the field of aeronautics was extremely simple. Think of this: what bird, butterfly or fish in whose image the aeroplane should be built, flies without a skin with bare bones and nerves? Where can you see a living creature carrying its innards on its exterior? Yet the old-time aeroplane did just that. Its heart lay on top with no protection at all. The wind moaned and whistled through its extensive rigging, clogged it with dust, soaked it with rain and dried it with sun. All those webs, strings and boards increased the surface area and its resistance tenfold despite their obvious lightness. Junkers decided to cover the aeroplane's nakedness, make a chest for the machine's heart and a tummy for its guts. Count Zeppelin's stupid sausages still occupied the attention of the public and the Imperial Court. Wilhelm, greatly fancying the scale and altogether militaristic look of those flying contraptions launched them into the air in whole packs while Professor Junkers took out a patent for the first machine made entirely of metal. The pilot and fuel tanks were both hidden inside a silvery-white oblong aluminium body.

The war brought the professor resources and world fame. Satisfied that he could at last work without worrying about the pennies, the kindly, humane Junkers who seems more like a vicar than a scientist, sent model after model and flight after flight to the fronts. His fighters became, after submarines, the favourites of Admiral Tirpitz. The buzzing of his silver dragonflies left an indelible scratch of fear in the memories of millions still alive and millions who fell.

After the Versailles Peace, the Entente commissioners ar-

rived in the quiet little town of Dessau and smashed up with hammers anything that might serve the aims of war. The plans for an
unbuilt torpedo-carrying plane went to Paris. The plant halted. At
the high noon of the inflationary crisis, Stinnes and AEG, the big
sharks, gathered in the murky waters around Junkers. Those were
the years when you could become the chief of any concern if you
were smart enough to send a couple of thousand dollars with your
visiting-card.

The professor had had enough experience with war department officials to have any illusions as to the fate awaiting him in
the pocket of a private businessman. The merchant is an enemy of
innovations not forced upon him by competition. He must make
the most of what already exists and milk as intensively as possible
an idea that has already won its market. It would not enter the merchant's head to compensate him for the experiments that had by
now swallowed up all the professor's means and all his government
grants.

At this tough moment God sent Junkers two guardian an-
gels to deliver him from the voracious jaws of the speculators: an aluminium pot furnace and Sachsenberg. First, about the pot furnace.
Every Don Quixote has his Sancho Panza. To enable the scientist's
thoughts to range freely, commit stupidities, make mistakes, drop
what has been started and begin all over again whatever the cost, a
docile devoted donkey of practical common sense must follow behind him. Its broad back will carry him out of any situation and on
days of setbacks will seek out its hero in a roadside ditch licking his
muddied face with the heavenly caress of its warm rough tongue.

A workshop for advanced aluminium smelters had nestled
on the fringe of the plant for a long time. In the days of the revolution when soldiers suddenly started ripping the epaulettes off their
smart lieutenants, this furnace emerged from its workaday garb; its
broad shoulders and industrious fists were extracted from the
wreckage of the frail aero-dragonfly. And to this day it tamely re-
pays all the professor's costly ventures into the land of the unknown.

After the war Germany's heavy industry suffered a major

crisis: the change to peace-time production. Krupp started making mincing-machines and milk separators; heavy Stumm, the battleship king, took up children's toys. The change came easier to Junkers's plant than to others. The Versailles Peace only made him expand in a new direction. That tiny bird of prey, fleetingly glimpsed as a scarcely noticeable spot in the sky of war, descended, grew bigger and its whole body was gradually reborn. Its head was enlarged, its trunk extended and its wings threw themselves out into a strong metallic cross. And, impelled by hunger, the eagle of war entered the service of the post office.

Was it alone? The waves of revolution rose high and white-haired people with thoroughbred noses had to live more and more badly. They joined foreign legions and were hired as soldiers by the little Baltic states. Deeply concealing their pride as officers of the Imperial Fleet it was they who begrudgingly did the dirty work of hunting down Bolsheviks for the Latvians and Estonians. But the governments of small shopkeepers and retainers had no intention of letting this picked guard of German imperialism make itself at home in their countries for ever. For Latvian peasants still remember the agrarian riots of 1905 and the country folk hanged by the ribs on the baronial lands; they remember the Ostsee bureaucracy, that bulwark of Russian autocracy, and the keys of the city of Riga handed over to Wilhelm II by the head of the Baltic nobility. In short, these *Landsknechte* were used and then booted right out. Thousands of German peasants who had been promised land and a house if they would make a little war on the Bolsheviks paid for the adventure known as the Baltikum with their lives.

In 1919 one of these detachments returned to Germany virtually on foot. The wolves that had been cut down in war decided to take up farming if only to avoid serving the cursed republic that to them still appeared to be revolutionary. They planted potatoes, carted muck and when they lifted their heads from the plough or spade they followed a Junkers mail plane flying over their fields with a longing gaze. Sachsenberg, the founder of a farm for officers and an organiser of exceptional ability, very quickly contacted Dessau and offered the professor his services and an elaborate plan for

international air lines. That select bunch from the old imperial offi-
cer-caste, hated by the proletariat and the finance aristocracy and of
no use to anyone at home, took to the sky. Russian emigres in Paris
are reputed to be first-class hairdressers, waiters and chauffeurs
especially. But these people were soon to become the best coachmen of the international sky, travelling the horizons of Europe and
Asia as calmly as the former did the Paris boulevards.

The commercial side of the business requires that the cit-
izen can board an aeroplane as easily as a lift or motor car. Aviation
must be dethroned and have all its romantic features plucked so as
not to scare off the shy bourgeois. That's why the modern aeroplane is so infinitely vulgar in its interior decor. Its armchairs have
been taken from the smoking-room of a bank, its mirrors trans-
planted from a middling restaurant and the whole cabin is full of
the habitual dusty luxury of the European railways. The toilet with
its white board on the door is soothingly familiar and utterly down
to earth; imperturbable, obliging paper bags for queasiness beckon
from their nails. So rare are accidents, so convenient the spittoons
and so calm the pilot's mittens on the control column that the passengers no longer offer him their hands. One more step forward
and he will be the equal of the servant and the chauffeur. The bourgeois will finally be freed from his fear when he sees an aviator in
livery. Flying will become ten times more popular the day they start
to accept tips in the air.

There is a special irony in the fact that this de-mystifying
and uncrowning of aviation has attracted the last romantics of the
old regime. With impassive faces they bring their machines up to
the 'apron' and then calmly wipe the traces of their passengers' sea-
sickness off the silver wings. There are among these men fliers who
had their legs torn off several times during the war: first their own
and then the wooden ones. Even now they carry them out of the
cockpit in their hands. Yet . . .

The land belongs to the republic. It has been cut out for
many years and divided up without any to spare. The stitches put in
by the Versailles Peace and Dawes will not be unpicked by a bayonet for the time being. But the sky, a great blue continent, is not
fully discovered or fully conquered. Here are unsounded depths and

untravelled roads through which no one has passed. Clouds crawl across it like opulent caravans open to plunder. And, morever, what has been already seized cannot be retained. Command of the air is a result of the changing balance of power. The very boldest flight does not leave a trace — not even the light strands of foam running after a ship across the ocean.

The great powers launch fleet after fleet into the air but their ships are for the present swallowed up in the world-wide expanse, minute in comparison with the millions of miles that have to be covered. The night sky is the setting for the new war; to shower Russia's snowy expanses with dynamite and nail China to the ground, the enemy's air forces have to stand like stars over the great agricultural plains.

Furrowing through a foreign sky Junkers planes are continuing to expand in empty space an empire that no longer exists. China has been lost, Kiaochow seized, the Baghdad railway torn from Germany's hands and the Congo gone. But there is China's sky, open to all winds. They can see the flag of the lost Pacific fortress hoisted on its clouds. High in the air hostile routes of the airways criss-cross and cut each other. The struggle for these colonies is only just warming up.

Junkers planes are winning them not for themselves nor for their country. The knots of Versailles bind them tightly. They work for any client and every customer.

Deruluft's* tentacles stretch into Italy, Scandinavia and Switzerland; Sachsenberg has conducted an offensive into the Balkans and through the Balkans into Anatolian Turkey.

Not so long ago Dessau began to stir like an alarmed beehive. Airmen who had flown in from all parts sat down gloomily at the table in their pub. Strictly by rank and by the list in the officers' mess. One has come back from Persia, another had come down on the Gobi sands while on a third is the dust and sunburn of a Russian summer.

"How's the health of the Crown Prince?"

* Deutsche-Russische Luftlinien — the joint German-Soviet airline operating in the 1920s. (R.C.)

"Very well, thank you, His Highness has bought a new horse."

"The King of Saxony . . ." But this is not the big news after which these men are usually prepared to chase and comb through the skies of the whole world. The bombshell bursts.

"Haven't you heard? Junkers has signed a concession with Poland. We are to build a fleet for those rascals." For a whole week the lieutenants drink dismally around the grail and with loathing set their coachmen's accounts in order: they measure out miles to the nearest yard — pieces of space chopped off infinity. There's nothing else to be done. Such is the law of capitalist development. Trade is a member of no party and internationalised.

Homeless German imperialism will run little fighters' nurseries for both its enemies and friends. Always hoping that the pupils will not grow too quickly into teachers, that its own people will, at the decisive moment, find themselves at the helm and that the shadow of machines built by these same German engineers will never hang over the fields of Germany. A vain hope.

The war industry of foreign countries is avidly learning from Junkers's pilots and designers. But scarcely having learnt to walk it is already driving from their command posts men in whom it senses irreconcilable enemies. Futile are all attempts to strengthen his position by honest and entirely disinterested work. The better the school the sooner the pupil reaches maturity and casts off his foreign tutelage. The more conscientiously Junkers fulfils his obligations the quicker they endeavour to be free of him. The gates of plants that he had built and put into operation one by one slam behind him. The self-assurance and youthful ignorance of his pupils only accelerates his collapse.

No one is enduring these catastrophes with as much pain as the professor himself. At the first disquieting telegrams he redoubles his efforts. He invests ever fresh resources into the threatened enterprises. This has brought him several times to the verge of ruin. Nevertheless, one fine day, embittered and once again unemployed aircraft builders will again appear on the doorstep of his quiet little house in Dessau.

Junkers is the purest scientist. For him air services are in the final count as necessary as the furnace. He runs them in order to nourish his experiments without perhaps suspecting the colossal political significance of the international organisation he has created. Of course he gives his contractors more than they him. For what is money compared with that culture of knowledge, experience and organisation that he scatters throughout the world like Mechnikov with his yoghourt.

But in the final analysis the professor cannot complain of lack of success. Under whoever's flags his ships may fly today not a single government has at its disposal such an integrated staff or magnificently trained, educated airmen, engineers and workers. Not one of his men had arrived ready-made. The majority began their service as volunteers, receiving no pay for months, suffering hunger and hardship. They grew up with their machines. Each step forward and every new invention was checked by them in practice. The pilots were a sensitive monitoring apparatus without which the professor could not have worked. How useful to him was even little Jüterbog, an indefatigable coachman of the air endlessly roving somewhere in the East. He flies low, hugging the earth tight. In stormy weather the Caspian Sea spits foam almost on to his wings, he creeps along through fogs, stumbling over the telegraph poles of the East India Company but there has never been an occasion when wind or fog has halted him somewhere en route. He roams on for days on end but he will without fail get his sack of letters and his two or three Persian merchants, yellow with the pitching, to their destination. That's Jüterbog and there's nothing he doesn't know about tropical dew, the finest desert dust and the effect of air, sun and humidity upon an aeroplane's organism.

Take another man: promoted from a mere mechanic to one of Junkers' most brilliant airmen today. He is not drawn to the East. He still circles round the lushest, dampest, cheeriest bit of Europe. An ex-sailor, he's happy in thick fog, on the damp wind of Holland. Over hundreds of miles through dense haze the golden fires of Amsterdam's taverns beckon to him. Mr. N. is a night pilot. His bulging eyes, flush with his face, can see in the dark. He can feel the nocturnal earth beneath him like the sea-bed under a fishing-boat. And he avoids danger with amazing sensitivity.

For speed and altitude records there are the cold idlers. They board their machines without changing their suits and emerge unstained. Formerly higher gentry, overfed with life, lovers of a risk that is frozen like a bottle of wine in the rarified atmosphere. For them the value of life can be equated with the maximum of acute, nervous pleasures still to be squeezed out of it. The result is immaterial. The object once achieved is not even worth talking about. Yet how delectable are those minutes of single combat at an altitude of 5,200 metres where danger lies dissolved in the air like a diamond in a glass of water.

But it is not in new air lines, nor in agents' offices and aerodromes, nor even in the main shops of the renowned aircraft factory at Dessau that the tap-root of the business lies. The heart of Junkers is hidden away in an unprepossessing little single-storied house standing apart from the commercial offices, where Sachsenberg and his lads run the business side and the aerodrome swept bare by the propellors' whirlwinds. Here is his scientific research institute, chemical laboratory and archive. Experts say that there is nowhere like it in Europe.

All the work of the scientists gathered here is founded upon the deepest mistrust of materials. Their laboratories are an arena where metals fight for supremacy like champions. Anyone can take part in the contest. From specimens from the best-known firms down to unheard-of young fighters coming on to the market for the first time. Krupp's proud steel must prove its advantages every day. The first chance tramp to be met on the street can challenge it to a duel. The metal that wins first prize in Junkers' modest laboratory will become a celebrity by the morning.

Bright white aluminium triumphed over all its rivals and only then would the professor decide to cast his aeroplanes from it. To date over twelve competitors are scrapping over the tough material for the engine, for a wheel that gives off heat more readily than others, an axle that does not snap on landing, a steady frame and a light wing. One metal shows off the skin of an eskimo fearing no amount of cold, another is a negro created for African heat.

Investigation of raw materials does not begin with the finished article but with atoms. The metal lies down under a microscope and then is shone through with X-rays. The slightest irregularity in the alignment of its crystals is enough for the whole batch to be rejected. Steel is a terrible thief. Minutes are sufficient for it to snatch up any alloys. A special gadget in the laboratory forces it to yield everything it has gathered up and concealed. Stolen carbon is burnt up in its stubbornly clenched fist.

Thus, over the years, absolutely priceless scientific material has been accumulated. The résumés of these experiments, each of which is strictly recorded, grow up into entire libraries. Outstanding scientists collate them. Before setting to work the young practitioner studies all the literature existing on the subject in question. He stands directly upon the shoulders of his predecessors.

No metal passes unrecognized through the monitoring section. Any alloy can, like a criminal by his fingerprints, be recognised by a little imprint inflicted with a ball in the testing apparatus. As strict as the party: materials that have passed the first purge are not exempted from the second. Every idea suggested, however persuasive it might be on paper, at once puts on its metallic body and defends it in practice. There are long thin pipes that have promised to sustain the whole weight of a wing. An unlikely load is lowered on to a fragile-looking reed. It withstands 9,000 kilos, over 40 per square millimetre, and fractures only after that. Steel veins twang on a torture rack: they snap at 5,200 kilos (50 per square millimetre). Mechanical scissors bite through threads used for sewing up parts of the apparatus. From thousands of skeins iron hands select the one that will take 127 kilos, 25 kilos per square millimetre of cross-section.

A metal in this department is like a sinner in hell. It is cut, ground, stretched, torn and snapped. A special machine does not let it go to sleep. Day and night it shakes the strips under trial, which, crazed with insomnia, tremble a light feverish tremble, the trembling of an aeroplane travelling at full speed. In another corner the spring of a skittle-like valve keeps squatting down and getting up for hours on end and an observer peers at its glowing core through a special tube and notes the slightest changes. Here all the accidents that could ever happen to an aeroplane are induced. The effect of any wear and tear and any catastrophe upon each individual component is calculated. Thousands of objects undergoing the effect of weight, heat, cold, impact and stress are in essence but one aeroplane dismantled into its smallest parts. This aeroplane makes a journey round the world, fights storm and fire, smashes, drowns and burns, experiencing a thousand most perilous adventures without moving from the spot or leaving the tiny laboratory.

The Chinese do not cherish their ancestors as much as the laboratory its bits of iron mangled during experiments. They are safeguarded in the most perfect order — set out along the path of aviation like a row of unforgettable warnings. An error can be corrected but science's retentive memory will for ever remain alert and attentive, if only because of one unsuccessful experiment out of a thousand successful ones.

The aeroplane is very young. Not even its life expectancy has been fixed yet. At Dessau there is a machine that has been flying since 1919 and no one knows how much longer it will hold out. What does it eat, what food is healthiest for its delicate constitution? For years chemists have hovered round fuel. But no supervision or warnings were of any help. So you have old men who have all their lives been led by the nose, deceived and duped by that frivolous, fickle petrol to whom in their old age has now come the idea of divorce. They have turned their glances towards the heavyweight, reliable, uncapricious diesel oil, towards those fatty liquors that the motor vehicle drinks in the Alps, Russian snows and Arctic ice.

"But," says the quiet little old man who reports every day to the professor on the behaviour of the oil in a jar, *"Das sind nur Anhaltspunkte, Wir wissen noch nichts!"* (This is only a basis. We still know nothing.)

Nothing? After so many years of toil, improvements and discoveries? Look at the scientist X-raying some microscopic mem-

brane and you suddenly go cold inside. How on earth did those first
men fly with no *Anhaltspunkte* apart from their own willpower?
Junkers has many courageous men but which of them would have
dared ascend on those wings of heavy iron now hung around the
walls like the hauberks of medieval knights?

With all its perfection Junkers's plant still resembles a university or a craftsman's workshop rather than a factory. Production
is hardly mechanised. The machine is the worker's spare hand, assisting and taking over one of his many actions but not carrying a
single operation through to the end. It is surprisingly difficult to
maintain strict uniformity of type using the hand. One rudder-cable
guide must be absolutely identical to the other; one claw under the
tail on which the machine rests when it lands should in no way dif-
fer from the other. The men cannot turn away from what they are
doing for even a minute. Their whole intellect is necessary for each
separate seam and every nut. The engineer with the close-set eyes,
flat face and infantry officer's cheek-bones can walk round as much
as he wishes and beat his brow against the unknown; let him track
down all items coming out of the workshop, rummaging through
and scrutinising them as if in a barracks. A worker's slightest negligence will lead to a catastrophe a day, a month or a year later. The
fear that goes with responsibility slows the work down dreadfully.
A man will sit for hours over a trifle and will not dare let it slip out
of his hands. The workers, engrossed, cultured and accustomed to
relying upon themselves, are becoming as individualistic as the airmen. Every little hammer speaks its own language. Bench-mates do
not understand one another.

Why was I reminded of the professor's house with its light
rooms full of the cries and scampering of children when in the very
section of the works where such a reverential stillness reigns and
only the scratch of a drawing-pen occasionally unpicks the silence
like a piece of taut silk? The children of Professor Junkers. You recall them not only in the drawing-office but even before, at the aerodrome where twenty machines lie out on an earthy meadow like the
plumage of swans. Not one looks like the next. Each has evolved
from its own embryonic idea and is not prevented from growing up

and testing its strength. A scientist's enormous patience is required
to rear children, machines and ideas the way Junkers does. Of
course it is hell for him at home. If one of the adjutants arrives with
a paper he has trouble finding a corner where the vivacious chatter
of the marvellous, self-educating, model children growing up as
their inner logic dictates does not reach. Any serious conversation
over the table is unthinkable. There is always an age at which any
situation seems madly comical. And the child dances a wild tribal
dance over his father's wise head. But take a look at this same principle in the drawing-office. A few dozen highly talented designers
hired only to think, draw or do nothing in front of their tables; they
are not daunted by their assignment. Any one of them can take any
detail or basic principle and stand it on its head. The works causes
an artificial selection of men unafraid of independent thought.

Among the taciturn drawing-boards before which the designers stand in white aprons like the anatomists of ideas, a font
has been set up for new-born ideas, a bureau that registers all the
findings. A meticulous clerk writes out the birth certificate of a new
idea as soon as the mathematician's heavy head begins to shine
through the light fabric of figures and formulas. This section regards as its most talented young engineer a former worker, an ap-
prentice who outjumped all his professionally qualified contemporaries in the feverish competitive race. He is a puny, mobile and unusually nervous man. In putting him on to one of the most responsi-
ble jobs Junkers was able to evaluate not only his talent but his
whole physiology which was imbued with a sharp aversion to brute
force and brute physical toil. No one will eliminate the remnants of
the aeroplane's animal nature with greater delight than the upstart
ex-worker who despises his 'low-brow' class. The future belongs to
brain. Aeroplanes, like engineers and scientists and all creatures of
the higher ruling stratum as a whole, should not have a body. So
there before him upon a wide sheet of Bristol board the final
touches are already being put to Junkers's pet idea: the machine has
been castrated, truncated and pruned. Its trunk, whether long like a
dragonfly's or short and fat like a bee's, has been reduced to nothing.

All the passengers, and the interior of the plane for that matter too, are hidden away in its wing, tucked under its arm.

In this shipyard of the air, these new fliers stand almost finished. Over them hangs the heady smell of paint and the day is not far off when, drunk with the spirits and oil which they are fed and rubbed down with during the final preparations, they are rolled out on to the field.

The bang of hammers resounds like a triumphal march: an armless machine tries on its wings and stands sensing for the first time the unprecedented weight, toughness and flexibility of its shoulders. Then, although not knowing what to do with them, it suddenly realises what the visible patch of sky in the square of the doorway means.

Workmen with nails between their teeth are still crawling through the empty eye-sockets in a skull which is upholstered with soft leather on the inside, while a pool of petrol is already lying on the bare floor.

It's peeing so it's alive.

Milk

With present-day unemployment and current price levels a German working-class family has to strain every effort to fight for its children's lives.

The drops of milk are counted out and eagerly sucked up if not every day then every other day and if it's not first grade then it's second grade. While they are drinking milk there is hope. It is only today that is wasting. The future sucks away at its fat teat and has rosy cheeks. In life's wretched game children are the last stake. Vaguely bound up with them is the idea of ultimately winning: 'well, if we can't our children will'.

The milkman's steps on the stairs of a reeking tenement are the steps of fate.

The milkman comes round at daybreak: the first herald of the day ahead. His ring gets people up from bed. They drowsily open the door to him wearing just their vests but without any embarrassment. The door may be open for only a minute. Through the narrow slit he can see everything: what left-overs there are from last night's supper, whether there is lard gone cold on the plates or a piece of stale bread on an empty oil-cloth, dirty beer glasses, the meagre sediment of acorn coffee — that illusion of food, the first substitute — or the thick pallid flabby-faced margarine that makes its appearance wherever money's coming in and the father or son is still working. The milkman casts one glance around the room. Aha! A heap of dirty washing in the corner, the stink of miners' boots drying out on the stove. To his nose that smell is sweeter than incense. They are working so they are living.

"I'll pour you first grade, shall I, Madam?"

And he's not wrong.

With sufficiency comes joy. Sometimes bare feet patter so gaily across the floor to the door, which is opened to the smart milkman with such a cheerful smile. What a disappointment! Warm sleepy eyes hit the bib of my starched apron as if it were icy armour-plating.

"Oh, Mr. Milkman, you are late today! I'm going to have a word with your neighbour. What's this then, you've got a new helper?" And the slam of the door echoes like a shot.

That was lyrical. In the majority of the flats there was nothing lyrical. At first sight it had seemed to me that the Essen miner or metalworker lives better than ours in Russia do. A collar and a stiff shirt front, clean shoes and a smart hat. Lunch in a tidy bag. It wouldn't hit you in the eye so much now that workers and peasants are getting more comfortable in our country. For us growing prosperity goes towards boots, fur coats, warm shawls and mittens. A heavy, shaggy, sheepskin-smelling comfort. In the West glittery department stores with their annual sales are at the worker's service. Mountains of smart, gaudy, hastily run-up rags. The price: five roubles a coat, 80 kopecks for stockings and three roubles for perfectly decent-looking boots. All these moult at the first rain, fade in the sunlight and have a mortal dread of air, wind and rain. The German worker will deny himself the most necessary things and go short on food and sleep if only to dress smartly and not stand out in the crowd by his poor clothes. His day-to-day requirements are infinitely more sophisticated than ours. For, as long as poverty does not break his bones in two he will not put on a dirty shirt or tolerate a bug or cockroach in his home.

"I think you wanted to meet a railwayman? Well, look, on the third floor they take six bottles of milk and one of cream. He's a *Lokführer* (engine-driver), twenty years on the railways; his old woman is a comrade of ours. Go on up, the old dog probably won't be back yet." And indeed he wasn't. A charming young lady opened the door.

"Comrade . . ."

Her unlined face, the face of a thirty-year-old girl who had not given birth or been close to the heat of a kitchen stove, an office-girl's podgy white face, winced and turned hostile:

"I'm not your comrade. Go and see mother, she's in the kitchen."

After the holes where I had only just been what a paradise this labour aristocrat's bright warm spacious flat seemed.

The kitchen was as white as snow. Shelves, chairs, cupboards, towels and table cloths — all snowy. An entrancingly fragrant cloud over the coffee pot, butter, ham and white bread on the table. A grand piano in the sitting room, paper flowers, curtains, a carpet, two magnificent beds in the bedroom, a mountain of feather-beds and, once again, snowy linen. Frau Rotte, the mistress of all this prosperity and abundance, was a stout but anxious woman of about fifty with a kindly face on which there leapt a neurotic flicker: her left eye twitched with a nervous tic. Her husband wasn't in. He had left behind him objects loathed by all the family: his old formal dress — a blue jacket with red cuffs and a sword presented to him for the quarter of a century's service that Frau Rotte would sourly say had 'made a man' of her husband.

Frau Rotte's unconscious communism had its origin at the time when she was roughly three years old and her mother, the widow of a labourer, left with little children on her hands, would on Sundays prepare to entertain the minister on whom she depended for financial assistance. As soon as his heavy steps sounded on the staircase the whole family would settle down around the Bible and start to sing psalms. That comedy went on for many hate-filled years.

Ever since then Frau Rotte could not look at a priest's clothing without shuddering. She married early and, as the local women said, couldn't have done better for she married a *Lokführer*, a man of honest, sober, steady character in good standing with his boss. Depression gripped her after having the first children. Her husband religiously brought home all his pay keeping nothing back for himself. Notwithstanding those visiting days at the clinic which he never missed Frau Rotte was left with a feeling of such bitterness and frustration that even thirty years later she could not forgive. Herr Rotte held the whole family in an iron grip. He would drive to church and on Saturdays wouldn't let them have a single newspaper. At times it seemed to Frau Rotte that she was re-living her mother's life. The footsteps of the parish vicar resounded continually in her head. Old Rotte drove his sons to their education with his fists and lash. They all ended up as accountants and technicians. Heinrich handles all the correspondence at Mannesman's. Otto is a cashier with a big bank. All of them are loyal servants to their masters — any class instinct firmly stamped out by their father's heels — pen-pushers for whom the sight of a worker's jacket arouses nothing but revulsion. Back in wartime Heine had made an attempt to go along to some workers' meeting. The poor lad forgot to take off his monocle, which he really did wear for short-sightedness, and was beaten up. He never forgave his class the misunderstanding and did not resume his coy attempt to return 'to his own'. For long years Frau Rotte had quietly watched her husband crippling, politically emasculating and selling her children one by one to the employers. Only in 1917 did she quite by accident run into a communist meeting, take a gulp of revolution and come home drunk on it. It was now too late for the older children. But she did save her youngest son: she made him into an ordinary metalworker and sent him to the Young Communist League.

Since then the old Rottes had an agreement not to argue about politics over the table in order to preserve the family. But the loss of the daughters causes the old woman untold pain. In this family which shows a cross-section of the social stratification of the highest-paid workers, the girls represent all the bourgeois republics from Scheidemann to Seeckt. They hate their father who has not given one of them an education. They hate his monarchy and his uniform, his voice and his fist.

But mother's communism is likewise infinitely amusing to them. Their father's broad back has after all lifted them up and set them down on the next rung of the social ladder. They have not swallowed factory fumes or choked over black bread. Admittedly a boss treats his typist no more courteously than he does a labourer. The beautiful girl who can type in three languages and knows book-keeping is out of a job today because she dared to rebuff an overture by her chief.

Mother sought to exploit her sorrow.

"Come with me to the meeting!" Minna just stiffened her smooth, still fresh neck.

"You get such horribly ordinary people there, mother. A girl who can earn 125 marks can't allow herself such idiocies. No, it's better for me to go to a cafe!" And then the old woman lost her temper and with a feminine sensitivity struck her in the most painful and well padded place:

"You're thirty now, just you wait and in five years you'll be finished. None of those rich people'll marry you. You're waiting for nothing. You don't want to marry a worker. But soon workers won't want you either. You'll be pattering round from office to office like a lone dog. You've fallen between two stools. And then, go and see yourself in a mirror — tired, grey and played out. A plain jaded charwoman like any other. You're worse than your father. The old man's got some sort of convictions even if they're false. But you've nothing. You'd be quite happy to give up the work you despise so much, and your body what's more, just for someone to call you in the dark *gnedige Frau* quite unintentionally. But they won't! You'll go to bed a worker and get up a worn-out hide."

"Du Klassenlose!" (You traitor to your class!)

That's the strongest abuse one worker can throw at another. Through the powder on her mealy-white cheeks a blush rises . . .

Appendix

Larissa Reissner

by Karl Radek

We are now approaching the tenth anniversary of the day when in a dark night for mankind the red star of the Soviets rose over the trenches of war. Out of the gunfire, the blood of the fallen, the sweat of munitions workers and out of the sufferings millions who wondered what the purpose of those sufferings was, the October Revolution was born. The roar of artillery and the yelping of the bourgeois and social-democratic press tried to drown it; but it stood firm and unwavering and all mankind timidly turned its glance towards it: some with blessings and hopes; others with curses and calumnies. It was the boundary between two worlds: a world perishing amid filth and a world being born in turmoil. It was a touchstone of the spirit. All that had been the 'spirit' of the bourgeois world – not only its priests and scholars, not only its writers and artists but all the 'intellectual' elements in the labour movement and that meant the vast majority of those bourgeois intellectuals who had condescended to 'save' the proletariat – all of them took fright at the countenance of proletarian revolution. People like Kautsky, Plekhanov and Guesde who had been invoking revolution all their lives, now turned away from it.

The section of the western European intelligentsia that

took a sympathetic attitude to the October Revolution saw in it only an end to the war, a revolt against war. Only a few saw in it the beginning of a new world and saw this trembling with excitement. In Russia only a minute portion of the intelligentsia joined the Bolsheviks. Russian intellectuals, even counting those who, like Gorky, stood close to the proletariat, could not envisage how this backward country could breach the front of world capitalism.

Among the few who resolutely joined forces with the proletariat in struggle with a deep awareness of the world-wide significance of what was taking place, an unassailable faith in victory and a cry of ecstasy was Larissa Reissner. She was only twenty-two when the death knell of bourgeois Russia struck. But she was not destined to see the tenth anniversary of the revolution in whose ranks she had fought courageously and whose battles she had described as could be described only by one in whom the soul of a great poet was joined with the soul of a great warrior.

A number of articles and small books – that is all of Larissa Reissner's literary legacy. Her one theme is the October Revolution. But as long as people fight, think and feel and as long as they are drawn to find out 'what it was like' they will read those books and will not put them down until they have reached the last page for they have the smell of revolution about their breath.

It is not yet time to write the biography of this outstanding woman. Such a biography would include not just gripping pages from the political history of the October Revolution but would also need to probe deep into the history of the cultural life of pre-revolutionary Russia and the history of the birth of the new man. Here I can only jot down a few thoughts which may serve as guidelines for such a work.

Larissa Reissner was born on 1 May 1895 in Lublin, Poland where her father was a professor at the Pulawa Agricultural Academy. Her father's Baltic-German blood mingled happily with her mother's Polish blood, the heritage of several generations' training in the German legal profession combining with the fiery passion of Poland.

She was brought up in Germany and France where her father travelled on professional business and stayed later as a political exile. In her parents' home a bitter spiritual conflict took place before her eyes.

From a conservative lawyer and monarchist her father turned himself into a republican and a socialist. The environment in which Larissa grew up changed abruptly. Russian professors were replaced by the German democrats, Barth and Träger and the social-democrats.

The little girl's clever sharp eyes spotted many things. She saw Bebel and the jolly Karl Liebknecht whom Professor Reissner as chief consultant in the Konigsberg trial, had to meet often. Throughout her life Larissa would recall how she would go round to visit 'Auntie' Liebknecht. The steaming coffee-pot that would appear on the table during such visits and the shortbread to which 'Auntie' would treat her – she could recall all this as if it were yesterday. These recollections formed the basis for the warm affection that Larissa nurtured towards Germany. The workers' children in Zehlendorf whom she went to school with, the tales of Theresa Benz, the working-class woman who helped her mother about the house all lived on in Larissa's memory so that in 1923 when staying illegally in Berlin in a worker's family she felt at home there. Both the old domestic help who used to wash her hair and her granddaughter whom Larissa would go out with to the Tiergarten saw her as a human being and not some foreign intellectual.

The first Russian revolution, whose waves rolled across the German frontier, found a response in the little girl's soul. Father and mother maintained constant friendly contacts with Russian revolutionaries in exile. Of course the little lass could not have known that Lenin's letters to Professor Reissner would subsequently become a source of pride. The comrades who appeared and disappeared mysteriously naturally stirred her imagination more deeply. When the 1905–1906 revolution came her father could go back to Russia and Larissa found herself in Petrograd. So far the path had lain straight towards the revolution. But here it turns aside: and yet it is striking how she was never really diverted from the true road, the road of her whole life. Her father, a professor of constitutional law and a Marxist, entered into a struggle against the liberal circles of professors at Petersburg University. The great world of learning is essentially a tiny world of learned men. Therefore there is no muck, pettiness or meanness that great scholars will not use against an enemy. They become suspicious of the socialist and of what do you start suspecting a socialist? Why, of course, of being a secret agent of the reactionaries. The old gossip-monger Burtsev, latched on to this bit of slander and had in addition his own private grudges. For years Professor Reissner struggled for his political honour, against the 'one-eyed monster' from Peer Gynt, against slander, myths, whispering campaigns and insinuations that could not be challenged or brought to legal proceedings. He leaves political life. In the home, need, worry and, finally, bitterness and despair take over. The little girl, being closely attached to her parents with bonds of love, understood perfectly well why their home was becoming emptier, her father's voice was heard less and less often and why he paced up and down for hours. Such recollections left a deep mark on her heart and although they built a wall between her and revolutionary circles they did not distract her from questions of socialism. While still at secondary school where her stay was a real agony for the lively talented girl, she writes the play *Atlantis* (published in 1913 by Shipovik) which, although not consistent in form, already indicates the direction of Larissa's ideas. She portrays a man who, by his death, wishes to save society from its doom. A child's play! A 'man' can never save society from doom. But the girl who had written this play had sat up in bed for many nights pondering mankind and its sufferings. The theme of this first work of Larissa's comes from Poehlmann's *History of Ancient Socialism and Communism*. This is all the more interesting in that at that time Larissa had fallen under Leonid Andreev's direct influence. That major individualist writer was not only her literary tutor but also influenced her spiritual development. But he could not divert her from the path that she had chosen for herself. Neither he nor the poets of the Acmeist circle, like Gumilev who had influenced her in form, could do this.

In 1914 when all these poets became the Tyrtaeuses of the imperialist slaughter, without a moment's hesitation she and her father came out in defence of international socialism.

They pawned their last belonging to obtain the means to publish the journal *Rudin* and start a fight against the traitors to international solidarity. Only the political isolation of the Reissner family, who were perfectly well known to the security police, accounts for the appearance of such a journal. Otherwise the malicious caricatures of Plekhanov, Burtsev and Struve would have been enough to have it closed down. The struggle against censorship and financial hardship was conducted by the 19-year-old Larissa. Inside the journal she likewise conducted a struggle of ideas with brilliantly cutting verse and sharp sarcastic comments. But this struggle had to end. Like any war it required money and they had no money. When there was nothing left to pawn, the journal ceased to exist. Larissa started collaborating on *Letopis*, the only legal internationalist journal at that time.

From the first moment of the February Revolution Larissa sets to work in the workers' clubs. Besides that she writes for Gorky's *Novaya Zhizn* which, while not deciding clearly to advance the slogan of Soviet Power, did wage a campaign against the coalition with the bourgeoisie. Her piece against Kerensky showed that thanks to her acute artistic sensibility she could at once appreciate the decaying hollow nature of Kerensky's government. Her terse jottings and sketches describing the life of the workers' clubs and theatres in the days leading up to October are most interesting. In those sketches you are struck by her deep understanding of the masses' natural urge for creative activity. In the awkward attempts by workers and soldiers to represent life on a stage, which the arrogance of the intellectuals found a subject for contemptuous sneering, she could perceive the emergence of the creative efforts of the new class and new social layers that wished not only to perceive reality but to represent it and pass it on. Her profoundly creative nature sensed the creative impulse of the revolution and she followed its summons.

In the first days after the October Revolution she worked

on assembling and cataloguing art treasures for the museums. As a connoisseur of art history she helped save and preserve much of the legacy of bourgeois culture for the proletariat. But now the first battles against the counter-revolution began. We first had to defend our lives and our right to exist so as to lay a foundation for the future creative work of the revolution. Having joined the party Larissa now leaves for the Czechoslovak front. She could not be a mere onlooker in the struggle between the old and new worlds. She serves at Sviyazhsk where the Red Army was forged in the battle against the Czechoslovaks. She takes part in the struggle of our Volga fleet. But she does not tell of this in her book *The Front*. There she relates the battles of the Red Army, passing modestly over her own role. So another participant in those battles, Larissa's comrade, A.Kremlev, must tell us about her. On the occasion of her death he wrote the following in *Krasnaya Zvezda*, organ of the Revolutionary War Council:

"Before Kazan. The Whites sweep all before them. We learn that at Tyurlyama the Whites have broken through in our rear, wiped out the sentries and blown up eighteen wagon-loads of shells. Our sector is cut in two. The Staff is here but what has happened to the men cut off?

The enemy is moving towards the Volga, in the rear of not only our detachment but of the flotilla as well. Trotsky's train was stuck near Sviyazhsk.

Order: slip through, locate and establish contact with those cut off.

Larissa goes off taking Vanyushka Ribakov, a sailor lad (a boy!) and someone else I don't recall and the three are off.

Night, shivering with cold, loneliness and the unknown. Yet Larissa was marching so confidently along that unfamiliar road!

At the village of Kurochkino somebody spotted them, they are fired on, they spread out, it's hard to crawl – a tight spot! And Larissa is joking and her hidden anxiety only makes her voice more velvety.

They slipped out of the line of fire and they were through!

'Are you tired, my lad . . . Vanya ? And you ?'
Through her concern she reached an unattainable height in that
      moment. They wanted to kiss that marvellous woman's
      hands black as they were with the grime of the road.
She walked along quickly with long strides and they almost had to
      run so as not to lag behind her . . .
And by morning at the base of the Whites. Charred ground,
      corpses – Tyurlyama.
From there, almost dropping on their feet, they made for Shikh-
      rana and where the Red Latvian regiment was positioned
      and contact could be made with Trotsky's train.
The front had been tied up. And that woman with the wan smile
      was the knot of that front.
'Comrades, look after my boys. Me ? – no, I'm not tired!'
Later, scouting by Verkhnii Uslon, near the two Sorkvashes and as
      far up as Pyany Bor. Eighty versts on horseback without
      flagging !
In those days pleasures were few enough. Yet the smile never left
      Larissa Mikhailovna's face in those tough campaigns.
And then Enzeli, Baku and Moscow !
And that was what a sailor from a landing-party recalled."

On the campaigns the sailors came to love her warmly and
as one of themselves because her courage was combined with a
naturalness and humanity; there was no falsity in the masses'
attitude towards her for it never entered anyone's head that at the
front she was not only a comrade-in-arms but the flotilla comman-
der's wife – she had married Raskolnikov in 1918. In just the same
way while she was a commissar at the Naval Staff Headquarters in
Moscow in 1919 she knew how to establish and maintain excellent
and friendly relations with the naval specialists, Admirals Altwater
and Behrens. Her good breeding, sensitivity and tact would not
permit the admirals from the Tsar's fleet to feel that they were under the control of an outsider.

In 1920 she travels to Afghanistan where her husband had
been appointed plenipotentiary. She spent two years at an Eastern

despot's court taking the obligatory part in glamorous diplomatic occasions, playing a diplomatic game in a struggle to influence the Emir's wives. 'Glamorous' if dirty work in which it would have not been hard for a young woman cut off from the struggling proletariat, to have become divorced from the revolution. But Larissa Reissner is reading serious marxist literature. She studies British imperialism, the history of the East and the struggle for freedom in neighbouring India. Away in the mountains of Afghanistan she feels herself a particle of the world revolution and prepares for a new struggle. Her book *Afghanistan* shows how her horizon is broadening and she is turning from a Russian revolutionary woman into a fighter in the international proletarian army.

In 1923 she returns to Soviet Russia. The land of workers and peasants has now a totally different aspect from when she had left. The stern Spartan war communism that had seemed to be a direct leap from capitalism to socialism gave way to New Economic Policy. Larissa understood, as we all did, the necessity for such a step. Scope had to be given to the business initiative of the peasant not just to obtain the raw materials for industry but if only not to die of starvation. Larissa understood this in theory. But could you arrive at socialism by this route? The answers that she and the party could provide could not still her inner anxiety. She realised that it was impossible to go on with the old regime of war communism. But in her heart of hearts she yearned for a heroic attempt to break through to the new social order with arms in hand. Yes, of course the streets of our towns had come back to life. Lorries laden with goods, shops open, factory hooters calling people to work, but perhaps the bourgeois elements will grow stronger besides ourselves? Will we be able to cope with them? Will our industrial managers, compelled now to engage in commerce, become infected by the poison of capitalist morality? Might the rot even reach the body of the party? Throughout the summer of 1923 Larissa is uneasy and looks around with an inward apprehension.

In September she comes to me with a request to help her go

to Germany. That was after the mass strikes against the Cuno government, at the time Germany's proletarian masses were once again seeking to cast off their chains. Poincaré occupied the Ruhr, the mark fell at breakneck speed and the Russian proletariat followed the German situation with bated breath. Larissa was itching to get there. She was itching to fight in the ranks of the German proletariat and make its struggle more intelligible to Russian workers. Her proposal pleased me greatly. Just as German workers were unable to gain a clear idea of what was going on in Russia, Russian workers thought of the German proletariat's struggle in rather an over-simplified and schematic way. I felt convinced that Larissa better than anyone else could establish a link between these two proletarian armies. For she was not a contemplative artist but a fighting artist who sees a struggle from the inside and knows how to convey its dynamics – the dynamics of humanity's destiny. Yet at the same time I felt that her trip to Germany was also an escape from unsettled doubts.

Larissa arrived in Dresden on 21 October 1923 at the point when General Müller's troops were occupying the capital of Red Saxony. As a soldier she understood the need for a retreat. But when, a few days' later, news of the Hamburg rising arrives, she springs to life. She wanted there and then to leave for Hamburg and grumbled about having to remain in Berlin. She whiled away many days at the shops among the crowds of unemployed and starving people attempting to buy a bit of bread for millions of marks and she sat around in hospitals packed with dead-beat working women deep in bitter thoughts and cares. At the time I was living clandestinely, meeting only party leaders who had no opportunity themselves to mix with the masses. Larissa lived the life of those masses. Whether chatting with unemployed in the Tiergarten, going on 9 November to a social-democratic requiem for the German Revolution or else attending a silver wedding party in a communist family, she could always find a way into people's hearts and always snatch up a piece of their lives. She lived among Berlin's working masses who were as close to her as the masses of St.Petersburg or the sailors of the Baltic fleet. She proudly returned from a demonstration in the Lustgarten where the Berlin proletariat had visibly proven the existence of the 'banned' Communist Party to General Seeckt and his armoured cars.

Larissa finally had the chance to go to Hamburg to describe and immortalise for the German and world proletariat the struggle of the Hamburg workers.

'After all that sluggishness and flabbiness you find here something solid, strong and vital', she wrote immediately upon arrival in Hamburg. 'At first it was hard to fight off their distrust and prejudices. But as soon as the Hamburg workers saw me as a comrade, I could learn about each and every one of their simple, great and tragic experiences.'

She lived with the abandoned wives of the Hamburg freedom fighters, sought out the fugitives in their hideouts, attended court hearings and social-democratic meetings. At night she would read Laufenberg, the historian of Hamburg and the Hamburg movement. The stocks of material she gathered in those weeks indicate how she worked – with a deep sense of responsibility and the feeling of a person for whom the smallest episode in that struggle had the sound of humanity's *Song of Songs*. Back in Moscow she spent many hours with one comrade who had led the rising and had been forced to escape. She checked over all this material with him and corresponded with comrades when doubts arose with regard to particular facts. The little book, *Hamburg at the Barricades*, was not written by a keen artist but by a fighter and for fighters. The German proletariat has given hundreds of clashes, battles and skirmishes to its enemies but none has been described with such love and deference as that struggle of Hamburg proletarians. Larissa treated those she loved with generosity and the worthy Reichstribunal was not wrong to order that slim little book consigned to the flames.*

---

*Elsewhere (in an article for the Encyclopedia Granat) Radek notes that 'an aesthete protested against the ban in the liberal *Frankfurter Zeitung* in view of the book's great artistic merit'. He also observes that *Hamburg at the Barricades* 'is a unique work of its kind for neither the Finnish rising or Soviet Hungary has produced its equivalent'. R.C.

Larissa Reissner returned from Germany unbroken by the defeat. In Hamburg she could see the fire beneath the ashes. She could see how defeat rears strong people for future battles. But she nevertheless learnt that a quick victory of the revolution could not be depended upon.

After her return to Soviet Russia she had to find out what was going on in the depths of the masses who in the final count dictate the course of history. And being a person with an immediate grasp of reality she could not gain such insight by reading and debates. She goes off to the industrial and coal-mining districts of the Urals and the Donets Basin. She goes to the textile region of Ivanovo-Voznesensk and to petty-bourgeois Byelorussia. She spends entire weeks in railway carriages, wagons and on horseback. Once again she lives in workers' families, goes down pits and takes part in meetings of factory boards, shop committees and trade unions and has conversations with peasants – daily, hourly. She is feeling a way through the gloom, lending an ear close to life. Her book *Coal, Iron and Living People* was the fruit of this work and here was a work tough both physically and morally which few writers have undertaken; yet it forms but a small fraction of what she experienced, thought and felt.

With this book begins a new artistic and ideological phase in the work of Larissa Reissner. In this work she, as a communist, takes a stand on firm ideological ground and finds her style as a writer. Her doubts disappear. She sees the working masses engaged in construction. They are building socialism, whether drenched in sweat at a blast furnace, descending half-naked down the pits or cursing their low wages while the best part of them are stoutly convinced that these torments and forced labour are all in the name of socialism. In a clumsy uncouth manager she recognises an old comrade from the front who here too has to tighten the reins with an iron hand but at the same time listen attentively to the masses to take all factors into account. She sees the colossal energy that the revolution has aroused in the deepest layers of the people and this strengthened her confidence that we could surmount all the difficulties connected with the revival of capitalist tendencies. She knows that the spontaneous petty-bourgeois element forms a swamp that can swallow up the greatest projects and sees what strange flowers blossom in this swamp. But she also sees clearly the path of struggle against the dangers menacing the republic of labour and the bulwarks with which the proletariat and the Communist Party can safeguard themselves. When she has gained this clarity and decides that her place is in that struggle she sets about sharpening her weapon. Her weapon is her pen. Hitherto Larissa has not thought much about whom she is writing for. She has an excellent knowledge of the history of literature and the arts and her style, rich and refined, reflects not only her keen power of observation but also the age-old culture that found such a fine embodiment in her. She is not however trying to be 'popular' for the working-class reader. She wants to create a fully valid work of art for the proletariat.

Larissa works a great deal at the end of 1924 and during 1925. She sits on Trotsky's commission for the improvement of the standard of industrial products. She reads many books on Russian and world economics. I will not pretend that she liked figures. When she had worked through two or three tedious text-books, she would implore me to give her something 'tasty' about petroleum or cereal crops and would relax over Delaisi's book on oil trusts or Norris's epic work on wheat. She was moreover making a thorough study of the history of the revolution. She prepared lectures on the 1905 revolution for the party cell at the armoured-car school; and when, after studying the specific material she came on to Lenin's articles of that period (1905–1906) she discovered greatness in the simplicity of our teacher's style and found the key to an aesthetic appreciation of his works that had formerly seemed too dry. Thus her art absorbed new elements. It is enough to read the descriptions of the Krupp plants and the Junkers works in her *In Hindenburg's Country* or her *Decembrists*. The first two descriptions are in a sustained technical style. That does not mean that she padded out her language with technical terms. But her interest in economics had taught her to think in a technical way. She perceives a machine or a factory building not just visually but as a concept. The style of

The Decembrists is influenced by a historical perspective. Here again though we do not have an imitation article nor an artificially archaic style. She sees the people in historical focus.

But history and economics for her were not ends in themselves. In them she investigates human inter-relations – how man lives and how he fights under specific conditions. Side by side with a colossal Krupp plant she sketches a miserable working-class barracks; in the Decembrist Kakhovsky she shows us a man 'insulted and injured' and draws a remarkable profile of the German jurist who had devised an ideal bureaucracy for the Tsar but ends his life in the snows of Siberia derided and forgotten. She shows us pathetic worms squashed by a giant of technology or the wheel of history.

Once matured as an artist and revolutionary Larissa Reissner prepared a new work. She conceived a trilogy about the life of the workers of the Urals: the first part about a serf factory at the time of the Pugachev revolt, the second on the exploitation of the worker under Tsarism and the third on the building of socialism. Simultaneously she was planning a portrait gallery of the precursors of socialism: not only portraits of Thomas More, Münzer, Babeuf and Blanqui but also portraits of the revolution's 'unsung heroes' starting from the first steps of the handicrafts proletariat and finishing with the titanic struggles of our day. At times she took fright at the tasks she had set herself. She was very modest and often doubted the power of her talents. But she would without doubt have accomplished these tasks for that power was growing with every new day.

But she was not destined to reveal all that was sleeping within her. She fell not in the fight against the bourgeoisie, where she had often stared death in the face, but in the fight against the nature she so passionately loved. When gravely ill, amid her last flickerings of consciousness, she exulted in the sun whose rays were sending her a last farewell. She spoke of how good it would be for her in the Crimea where she was going to convalesce and how lovely it would be when her weary head filled up again with new ideas. She vowed that she would fight for life to the end and she only abandoned that fight when she finally lost consciousness.

A number of articles and small books – that is all of Larissa Reissner's legacy. Articles scattered through newspapers and magazines, a few dozen letters all of which have yet to be collected. But they will live as long as the memory of the first proletarian revolution lives. They shall proclaim what the revolution meant for all peoples, for the West and the East, for Hamburg and Afghanistan, for Leningrad and the Urals. And this warrior woman in whose heart and mind everything found an answering chord will arise from her books after her death as a still living witness of the proletarian revolution.

A Most Absurd Death

by Viktor Shklovsky

It's very hard to write this. The past tense is so unsuitable for the dead woman. How can you write about a person when their accounting period has not closed. A most absurd death. There was Gorky in frock-coat and crew-cut. Sly, all-knowing Sukhanov. A quite young Mayakovsky. Today there aren't such young people.

Then there was Larissa Reissner.

With blond plaits. A northern face. Shyness and self-assurance.

She wrote reviews for *Letopis* and a verse-drama which was, as it had to be at the age of nineteen, of world-wide significance, *Atlantis*, I think.

We were then moving into the world as into a new flat.

Larissa Mikhailovna adored skating. She liked people to see her at the rink. And then she was working on the very amateur student magazines *Rudin*, I think it was, and *Bohem*.

As a writer, Reissner matured slowly, like a northerner.

Then the revolution. Like wind in a sail.

Larissa was among those who took the St.Peter and Paul Fortress. Not a difficult assault. But the fortress had to be approached. To have the faith that the gates would open.

The first meeting of *Novaya Zhizn*. Reissner was saying

something or other. Steklov was horrified and kept asking people near him: 'Is she a marxist ?' And at that time Larissa Mikhailovna was already taking part, I believe, in the Russian spelling reform.

Then she was not a thinker, she was twenty-two. She was talented and dared to live. People think they are eating a lot of life when they're only sampling it.

Reissner was greedy for life. And in life she filled her sail ever wider.

She tacked her course close to the wind.

She could describe the Winter Palace very well. She could see its comic side. She was with the Bolsheviks when to us they seemed a sect. Blok had said bitterly: the majority of humanity are 'Right S.R.s'.

I remember Larissa Mikhailovna at the Loskutnaya Hotel. She was then Raskolnikov's wife. The fleet was lying almost in the Moscow River.

It was almost embarrassingly crowded.

I was in the enemy camp. When I had re-considered things and come back Larissa greeted me as the finest comrade. With her benign northern bearing that was somehow good.

Then she went off to the Volga with the flotilla.

She eagerly packed up her life together as if strapping it all up to go off to another planet.

Raskolnikov's torpedo-boats slipped across the sandbanks and traced a red line along the Volga.

There on the campaigns Larissa Reissner found her literary style.

It was not a woman's style of writing. It was not the journalist's habitual irony.

Irony's a cheap way of being clever.

Larissa Mikhailovna held dear what she saw and took life in earnest. A little ponderously and overloadedly. But life itself was then as overloaded as a railway wagon.

Reissner grew slowly and didn't grow old. She didn't fully perfect her touch. The best things she wrote were done just recently. The fine descriptions of Ullsteins and the Junkers plants.

Germany she understood very well.

Here was a true reporter who did not see with editorial eyes.

The culture of a pupil of the Acmeists and Symbolists had given Larissa Reissner the knack of seeing things.

In Russian journalism hers is the style that has most left behind the style of the book.

That was because she was one of the most cultured.

That is how lavishly this journalist was created.

Larissa Mikhailovna had only just begun to write. She did not believe in herself, she kept re-educating herself.

Her best article is about Baron Steingel. (*The Decembrists* is, I think, only now being published.)

She had just taught herself not to describe or name her theme but to unfold it.

And that is the strange face in a familiar room at the Press House.

She was seen there so many times!

A living piece of Russian journalism seems to have been ripped away with the teeth.

Friends will never forget Larissa Reissner.

In Memory of Reissner

by Boris Pasternak

Larissa, now I start to feel regret
That I'm not death or nought compared with it.
I'd like to know how to these scraps of days
Life's chapters without glue so firmly stick.

Oh, how I had that raw material weighed!
Winters slumped back in heaps then downpours swept,
And with a blanket blizzards tightly swathed
Young suckling cities close against their breasts.

People on foot flashed past in wind and rain,
Trucks crawled round the first turn in the road,
Plunged to the neck in water were those years,
In floods across the shallows new ones flowed.

Yet ever more did stubborn life persist
In simmering in its still while nests were built;
Ringed round with street-lamps lay the building sites,
With starlight, words and reason they were filled.

Just look around, which one of us was not
From flakes and hazy reservations made?
For we were reared by some exquisite ruins
While you alone stand far above all praise.

And you alone, so well dislodged by strife,
Burst through in one clenched salvo to enthrall.
Had fascination not been known to life,
To answer it you'd be right on the ball.

You billowed up like some tempestuous Grace
Though scarcely lingering in her living fire.
At once lost mediocrity her face,
While imperfection too brought forth your ire.

In depths of legend, heroine, you'll walk,
Along that path your steps shall never fade.
Tower like a mighty peak above my thoughts;
For they are quite at home in your great shade.

In Memory of Larissa Reissner

by Lev Sosnovsky

Today as we remember Larissa Mikhailovna we must be absolutely frank. We have been unfair to her and I am one of those who has been unfair to her. She travelled her whole road among us as if passing through a whole succession of barriers where she was silently checked.

In our party circles which had come through the underground organisation frayed, ragged and unversed in the elementary conventions of civilised life, the figure of a thoroughly beautiful person who was refined from head to foot, in appearance, words and deeds, was alien. We had been so often deceived by those who came over to us that it was hard to risk disappointment yet again. So a silent, endlessly repeated, trial was held on Larissa Reissner that strangely transformed itself. I have all the more reason to speak about this as I had caught myself trying her on numerous occasions.

She passed the first test. That was when, without anyone driving or sending her, she was in those places where the fate of the revolution was really being decided. That was at Sviyazhsk, before Kazan. That was the first test. At that time she wrote little or else we seldom had a chance to read her.

After this when she joined our press and became a proper colleague of ours our second conflict with Larissa Reissner began.

We were all workaday and prosaic. In her there was much poetry, much emotion and much of the romantic. It struck us: wasn't there just too much elegance in her writings, weren't there too many images and too much colouring? At times it would strike us who were stumbling around in real life: was the object of her creativity just this continual juggling of colours, images, lines and juxtapositions?

When her sketches about Afghanistan appeared it was the third test. Wasn't this young woman being drawn towards exoticism? Was she turning her face away from our tedious prose and all-Russian greyness? Wasn't there here a private escape into the exoticism of bizarre lands and peoples? This was a new test.

Then there was Hamburg. After Hamburg the question was settled for me personally. Often we wrongly refrain from taking the steps we are in duty bound to take. I am speaking for and about myself. But perhaps I am also conveying the ideas, moods and thoughts of others. It was impossible not to have thoughts about Larissa Reissner because now there was no better journalist among us. Had each of us party journalists who had undergone that great revolutionary, organisational and practical party experience possessed her pen, her sense of colour and her sharp eye we could have done ten times or a hundred times more. If to this were added her education and her European experience – and that did not pass without trace – if all that had been added to our revolutionary Bolshevik temper we could have worked veritable miracles.

Therefore, assuming that I have not been alone in such thoughts and such a constant and strict testing of Larissa Reissner's work and worth, the moment that the test was completed we should have spoken to her about this frankly and fraternally. I don't know whether she would have needed this or whether she sensed a rather muted, very much suppressed and barely perceptible estrangement. Whether she did or not (I wasn't well enough acquainted with Larissa Mikhailovna to establish that) I do think that after Hamburg our duty was to come to terms with Larissa Mikhailovna openly and fraternally. It is harsh that this has to be done when she is no longer here.

After Hamburg I tackled her works quite differently. I saw that this person, in essence so young, had undergone before my very eyes such an enormous evolution. To embrace by the age of thirty such breadth of problems, fields, experiences and to have the courage to take up not just tiny deficiencies of a tiny apparatus but major deficiencies of a major apparatus, to take Krupps and probe it from the peaks of its secret boardrooms to the subterranean depths of its pits – all that was a test for a young intellectual that I doubt whether anyone else has passed.

When I approached her most recent work formally I no longer found that surfeit of images, beautiful forms and comparisons that distinguished her first works. This told me that Larissa Mikhailovna was working on herself very thoughtfully and rigorously. Perhaps even without that frank discussion I spoke about she sensed what our simple austere reader required of her. So she went to meet him.

I have previously mentioned in an article of mine one of her last newspaper sketches 'Milk' published in *Gudok*. In this sketch there was something quite new. Those who have had the chance to read this sketch will have seen yet another stage in the creative work of Larissa Mikhailovna. Whereas much of her earlier work dealt directly or indirectly with heroic aspects of life here you have a terribly oppressive prose, the life of the lower depths of capitalist society crushed beneath the burden of the Versailles Peace and its ramifications. Here there was only prose and no heroism. People fading away in poverty. But Larissa Reissner adopted this device. She takes us around with the milkman who goes up the stairs of a tenement at first light and takes us through different grades of poverty of Essen workers. This new, simple clear, bald device showed me that we still do not know even a small part of Larissa Mikhailovna's capabilities. And if there were still any doubts left then her recent fragments of an apparently large-scale work being projected on the Decembrists showed us quite new horizons for Larissa Mikhailovna. Her two sketches about the Decembrists published in a newspaper were like an advance put down for something very great to come. Those who are familiar with the attempts at artistic portrayal of real historical events that exist in our literature will know how in the majority of cases these historical fictional chronicles are vulgar, flat and false. In those two little sketches there was no longer a columnist or a newsman. Here was a great artist and a great creator.

When I read her sketch about Trubetskoi I personally thought Larissa Reissner was really a guest writer in a newspaper. For it was only her revolutionary fighting temperament that linked her with the newspaper. Even in her previous fragments about Ullstein and others you felt as though she was being drawn towards a larger scale. And that foretaste of something great also showed us that she was all the more a visitor – this is meant only in the finest sense of the word – to the newspaper and she had to give the country and the world something greater (whether she would have left newspapers or not I don't know) because if she could depict to us the full stature of a man who is separated from us by a hundred years what images could she have given of our era, the people she saw, felt and understood down to the last wrinkle. And here is the true cause of our grief and our great sorrow: it is that Russian and world literature has lost Larissa Reissner.

I mean world literature. Here there is no exaggeration. Today there should be no reason or need to say this. Many people think, and this is partly correct, that the ephemeral newspaper and the labours of the newspaperman represent something supremely transient and lightweight that disperses into the air like smoke. Yes, that is true. But only with regard to eras that are in themselves trivial, grey, pale and monotonous. But newspapermen who live and describe great eras, those newspapermen do not die so quickly. So that if they can learn faithfully and sincerely how to imprint just a small piece of their great era then they will conserve the breath of that era from decay and it will live on for many years.

In my quest for a model for the newspaper sketch, I once stumbled upon a book, a collection of sketches, by a certain Spanish journalist who lived in the 1830s. In liberal circles in Russia there were people who gathered together this Spanish writer's sketches which were so useful for inculcating the civic spirit in pre-revolutionary Russia and re-issued them. I read them over in an effort to understand what in his day was so powerful about this writer who commanded such popularity. Apart from boredom I could get nothing from them for the events he described were a miserable ripple on the surface of some puddle compared with the storms Larissa Mikhailovna lived through.

Our era needs to establish some harmony in the souls of its journalists with the whole key of the era. Perhaps that is an unhappy choice of words but I think that what identified and typified Larissa Mikhailovna can be defined by a crude combination of words: *a wild passion for life*. A genuine indomitable passion for life, an unquenchable thirst to be in Hamburg and in Essen and in the Urals and in the Donbass and in Afghanistan and in the Caucasus. And precisely because there was in this person such a temperament and such a wide range of interest in life, every line of hers irrespective of how we treated her, stirs people. In many years' time, if people then wish to feel something of the breath of the revolution and the breath of the great year of 1918 they will gain much from the works of Reissner. Think to yourselves: do you find very much vivid imaginative literature about 1918 that can be compared with Larissa Reissner's sketches? However hard I try to recall anything similar I can think of nothing. A true estimate and a true test cannot be expressed in our words but in the words of those who will think of the great era of our revolution with awe and will commune not with dry facts and chronologies but with the soul of that era. It will be such people who will give a true, impartial authoritative appreciation.

Larissa Mikhailovna Reissner's work on newspapers and her presence on the newspaper staff made us – newspaper labourers as compared with that great craftsman in style – somehow more wary and tense. How can you treat style and form with disdain when sketches like Reissner's are printed alongside your own? Even someone who never thinks especially much about form starts to reflect. For my part let me say that none of the seekings of the Formalists (i.e. the advocates of formalism in literature) have made any impression on me. But the last articles of Larissa Mikhailovna Reissner made me learn a thing or two. I believe too that more than one generation of pupil-trainees at the State Institute of Journalism will learn the model of a good revolutionary style from her sketches.

The main thing I want to say now is that we should help other comrades and friends to ponder the fact that for several years, too many years, we have been rather unfair towards her. Can this be put right by such a belated admission? Of course not. But it will perhaps help us to be more just and create a better atmosphere in future for those other workers as uniquely skilled as Larissa Mikhailovna Reissner.

Rosa Leviné-Meyer

Inside German Communism

Memoirs of Party Life in the Weimar Republic

Edited and introduced by David Zane Mairowitz

Rosa-Leviné-Meyer knew and lived amongst some of the most
powerful figures of the Communist world of the 1920s: Radek,
Trotsky, Ruth Fischer, Willi Muenzenberg and Thaelmann. Her
first husband was Eugen Leviné, hero and martyr of the Soviet
Republic in Munich. She later married Ernst Meyer, a central figure
and occasional leader of the Young Communist Party of Germany
until his death in 1930.

Her memoirs span the experience of Communism in Germany
and Russia, 1920-1933. They reveal a world of immense political and
emotional stress as Stalin slowly encroached on the KPD and
destroyed its weak and divided leadership.